Brown Edge
Memories

Tea ladies at end of war party at the school
L to R: Mary Rolinson, Rose Rolinson, Annie Berrisford, Pat --, Mrs Eardley,
Mrs Goldstraw, Mrs Bettany, ?, Lottie Hayes, Anna Turner, Mrs Sherratt, Mrs
Hancock, Betty Mitcheson, Mrs Horne, Frank Simcock

Compiled by Elizabeth Lawton

CHURNET VALLEY BOOKS
1 King Street, Leek, Staffordshire. ST13 5NW 01538 399033
www.leekbooks.co.uk
© Elizabeth Lawton and Churnet Valley Books 2006
ISBN 1 904546 45 5 (978-1-904546-45-0)

I would like to thank all the Brown Edgers listed in the front of the book who allowed me into their homes and shared their memories with me. I would also like to thank Clive Proctor, Catherine Jones, Joy Tatton and Ethel Dawson for additional material.

I feel these memories are important social history. They remind us how so much changes in a lifetime.

I am very grateful to my son John for all his work on the photographs and to Jane for processing all my scribbled notes.

I apologise for any errors and I hope that readers will have as much pleasure from these memories as I had in recording them.

Elizabeth Lawton June 2006

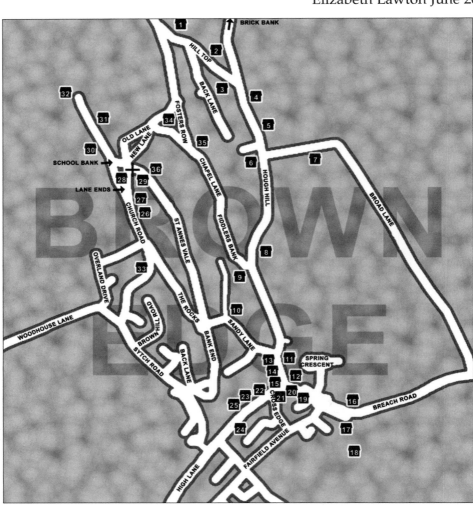

1. STAR FARM	13. PART OF WESLEYAN CHAPEL	25. GARNERS SHOP
2. FIRST PRIMITIVE CHAPEL	14. NEW INN	26. FIRST INFANTS SCHOOL
3. ROSE AND CROWN	15. ROEBUCK	27. VICARAGE
4. FREE MISSION	16. BREACH CAFÉ	28. JOE'S SHOP
5. COLLIERS ARMS	17. ROCK COTTAGE	29. GRANNY HEATH'S SHOP
6. HARVEY'S MISSION	18. ISOLATION HOSPITAL	30. UPPER STONEHOUSE
7. STEINFIELDS FARM	19. POOLFIELDS HOUSE	31. LITTLE STONEHOUSE
8. FERNYHOUGH FARM	20. FIRST POST OFFICE	32. LOWER STONEHOUSE
9. FOAMING QUART	21. LUMP OF COAL	33. SINGLET HOUSE
10. APPLETREE FARM	22. SHORT STREET	34. NEW LANE FARM
11. WESLEYAN CHAPEL	23. HOLLYBUSH	35. PRESENT PRIMITIVE CHAPEL
12. BRATT'S BUTCHERS	24. BAND ROOM	36. Y.M.C.A. THE TAB

Contents

Collecting water from the Sytch Well in Brown Edge in 1890.

COVER PHOTO
Kitty Clowes' grandfather Charles Hargreaves, centre, aged 79 in 1934.

A view of School Bank and the Vale showing the extensions to the school on the right. It also shows the YMCA (TAB) which was later demolished and a bungalow built on the site.

A very interesting view of the village taken from The Rocks. Sandy Lane is in the foreground. Short Street, which was just three little cottages, can be seen. It is interesting to see all the little haystacks on the smallholdings.

Samuel Dawson alias 'Razzor'. His recollections recorded by G.H. Heaton in March 1904

Samuel Dawson was born in June 1832, in a thatched cottage at Lane Ends, Brown Edge - a short distance from where the Church now stands, the youngest son of a family of 10 children. His father, Thomas Dawson, a collier, married Elizabeth Mountford of Fernyhough.

There being in those days no Education Acts to enforce the attendance of children at school, Samuel was sent to work at Norton Pits when only 7 years old, being employed under a 'butty' - Thomas Sheldon - at Mr Deane's Colliery. Here he worked for Sheldon, at small wages, until he was 21, afterwards continuing at the same colliery up to the time it was closed.

He next worked for Mr Robert Heath at Ford Green Colliery in the Cockshead seam, and subsequently at Ridgway, near Norton under Mr Hugh Henshall Williamson, where he in time attained to the position of 'Butty'.

When the pits at Ridgway were closed, he gave up working under ground, and offered his services as keeper to Mr Thomas Smith, of Park Lane, Endon, with whom he found employment more congenial to his sporting instincts up to a recent date, when, unfortunately he was prostrated by a serious illness from which he is now suffering.

In his early days, Brown Edge enjoyed an unenviable notoriety by reason of the number of poachers who were located there.

When quite young, 16 or 17, he joined himself to a gang of these nocturnal marauders, who periodically visited the preserves of certain sporting squires at Basford, Consall, Rudyard, Bosley and even as far off as Warslow (Sir John Harper Crewe's) where they helped themselves to considerable quantities of hares and rabbits, by means of long netting, sometimes bringing back their spoil in trap-loads. Longsdon and Rudyard, he describes, as having once been noted places for hares.

For a while the game was played with impunity, though not infrequently the poachers had to fight their way out of an encounter with keepers. In those days the police were not invested, as now, with the powers of search, so once safely on the high road they were free from molestation.

But in the end, this kind of unlawful pursuit was to bring the subject of our sketch within the meshes of the law and into 'durance vile'. One dark night in November, 1856, Dawson with seven others raided the preserves of Mr Benjamin Bull, of Hillswood, near Leek. Whilst in the act of setting their nets, the poachers were surprised by an equal number of keepers and watchers, who moreover were accompanied by two fierce night dogs.

A desperate struggle ensued, the poachers using their knives to ward off the dogs, and eventually Dawson and three of his associates were secured, the other four getting clear away. One of the keepers had his arm broken during the fray, but no firearms were used. Taken to the police station at Leek, they were next morning brought before the Bench and committed for trial at the Stafford Assizes. For one month they lay in Stafford Gaol awaiting their trial, and in the result they were found guilty - Dawson and two others, T. Goodwin and Adam Clowes, receiving a sentence of four year's penal servitude, and the other prisoner, S. Sheldon, who had previously been in trouble, six years.

The name of the Judge, who tried the case, Dawson does not remember, but describes him as the 'fou'est' (ugliest) man he ever set eyes on. Possibly, however, the terror of the law may have distorted his vision, so that he could not rightly take in the surroundings.

The first twelve months of the sentence was served at Wakefield Gaol, where the making of cocoa-nut fibre door mats was the chief industry, and the remaining three years at Chatham, where the prisoners were chiefly employed in scraping and painting an old ship, always under supervision of armed warders. It is to be noted that during his incarceration, Dawson had his first opportunity of learning to read and write. With his release, his career as a poacher came to an end and he never afterwards went out.

After his liberation he called to see one of the watchers on that fateful night, John Kirkland of the White Lion Inn, Leek (with whom he afterwards became on friendly terms) and found that Kirkland's dog, which had succumbed to wounds inflicted by the poachers' knives, had been stuffed and placed on the landing of the stair-case. Dawson adds that 'many a time has he patted that (stuffed) dog's head'.

Having renounced this one branch of 'sport', he soon found other means of employing his leisure, and at once became renowned as a prize-fighter. Though somewhat short in stature, he was a man of immense strength and determination, and withal of quarrelsome disposition, especially when inflamed by drink.

His first lesson in the art of self-defence was gained in boxing matches at some of the shows which attended the local fairs at Leek and Burslem.

One of his earliest fights was with Dick Weaver, a collier of Smallthorne, and at that time a man of drunken and dissolute habits. After drinking together, the parties came to a pitched battle hard by the tollgate at the top of Smallthorne, and Dawson gained the victory.

After Richard Weaver's conversion, and when his fame as an Evangelist preacher had spread far and wide, Dawson became one of his warmest admirers and often sat under him, describing his eloquence as great and far-reaching.

Dawson's first great fight took place nearly 50 years ago at Leek, on the occasion of the Christmas Fair, against a butcher from Sheen, with whom he 'fell out' in a public-house hard by the present Smithfield. Having adjourned to the open space, after an hour's stiff encounter, Dawson had 'knocked his opponent all to bits'.

The officers of the law appeared to have been conspicuous by their absence, but a considerable crowd congregated to watch and encourage the combatants.

Another fight was with 'Harry the Cobbler' who worked for Noah Baddeley of Endon, and which took place at the Black Horse Inn, Endon, the result of a quarrel over payment for a pint of ale.

Fifteen rounds were fought in the backyard, and Dawson ultimately knocked out his man, though not before he had himself received some severe facial bruises, the Cobbler being a big upstanding fellow.

The Plough at Endon was subsequently the scene of another of Dawson's triumphs, when Dick Pass of Ball Green - who is supposed to have been brought over for the express purpose of picking a quarrel - responded to a challenge. The fight took place in the Bar Parlour, 15 rounds sufficing to bring Pass to a state of repentance. The doors which had been fastened at the commencement, were broken open just at the moment when Dawson had laid out his man, and the Landlord and Police Constable appearing on the scene promptly ejected the combatants and dispersed the onlookers, but no proceedings followed.

Perhaps the most romantic fight was the one between Dawson and Jack Tomkinson, a boatman of Stockton Brook, from the fact that it occurred at mid-night on the public road, beneath the silvery light of the moon, and when no spectators were assembled. Whilst it was in progress, a solitary policeman put in an appearance and endeavoured to separate the combatants, with the result, that with one accord they both turned their attentions to this hapless 'limb of the law' and bruised him sadly.

Dawson thought the time opportune for 'making himself scarce' and by way of diversion betook himself for a month's harvesting into the adjacent County of Cheshire. In the meantime, Tomkinson had been 'hauled up before the beaks' and fined £5 and costs. Nor was Dawson overlooked, for on his return from Cheshire, he was compelled to appear before Mr Bailey Rose (the Potteries Stipendary) when, but for the kindness of the policeman, who, by way of heaping coals of fire on his head, pleaded for him, the result of the interview might have been disastrous. As it was he escaped with the nominal penalty of 12/-.

In an open field at Milton, Dawson fought the redoubtable Dick Tipping who was reputed a good fighter and heavy hitter. At the end of 20 rounds, Tipping was led off the field very badly hurt, blood issuing from both his ears, and Dawson again received the congratulations of his supporters.

James Shenton, familiarly know as 'Jem-the-Miller' from the fact of his workings at Stanley Mill, who rather fancied himself as a bruiser, was the next to receive a challenge from Dawson's friends, and once again Milton was the scene of action. After 17 or 18 rounds, Dawson records that he had closed both his opponent's eyes and left him much the worse for wear, whilst himself was as fresh as a daisy.

At Stockton Brook, Dawson met and defeated, after half an hour's tussle, George Mountford, alias 'Waggat', of Stanley Moss.

An encounter with Charles Frost, a boatman, took place outside the Lump of Coal at Sandy Lane, resulting from the usual quarrel and beer drinking inside. Here again Dawson held the upper hand, knocking Frost's head through the public house window, but not before he himself had received a 'sounder' or two - a small bone in his cheek being broken.

At Burslem Wakes, Dawson made the acquaintance of the celebrated 'Cabbage' from Talke-o'th-Hill. They alternately 'fell-out' and 'fell-in' all night long at the Red Lion, and finally at 7 o'clock the following morning adjourned to the backyard to settle their differences. In the first round, with a terrible right-hander in the neck, Dawson felled his opponent to the ground, where, having come in contact with an iron grating, Cabbage was at first thought to be dead, and Dawson was hurried off the scene of action by his friends all of whom were by this time thoroughly sobered. Fortunately, his victim soon came to himself, and as quickly made tracks in the opposite direction.

Dawson's last pitched battle, and the one in which, owing to adverse circumstances, he met with his first defeat, took place at Biddulph one winterly day at the beginning of March, against Jem Guy, a Shropshire man at that time living in Biddulph.

The stakes were for £5 aside and the fight, which lasted two hours (70 rounds being fought) attracted a large concourse of people. Quite early in the encounter Dawson had his arm dislocated (it had been previously broken and not properly set) and consequently had to fight single-handed, but not until he was fearfully bruised and exhausted did he throw up the sponge, and finally bid adieu to the prize-ring.

One 'pal' with whom Dawson had occasionally a friendly bout was 'Tank' Steel, a very big and active man, and Steel, he admits, in these skirmishes usually kept the upperhand.

In bringing these recollections to a close, the writer would especially state that they have been recorded <u>not</u> in any sense by way of glorifying Dawson's antecedents, but more for the purpose of conveying a warning, no one could apparently be more truly repentant than Dawson himself for the deeds of a mis-spent life, which now he would, if it were possible, gladly recall. As regards poaching, he emphatically observes that '<u>it is a bad practice and brings no one any good</u>'. Allowance must be made for the fact that he practically received no education, nor ever attended Sunday-school.

He entered married life when only 19 years of age, his wife being one Thomasin Simcock, and rejoices in a family of seven.

Asked whether his sons had inherited any of his unfortunate proclivities, Dawson's reply was 'Nay - they are very steady, and as 'quate' (quiet) as stones'. This I believe to be literally true.

G.H.Heaton

Samuel Dawson died in June 1904, about three months after these recollections were set down.

Samuel Dawson in Chapel Lane, c.1900.

Honor Benton (nee Honor Dawson)

Honor Dawson was born at Brown Edge in 1901 and lived at Brookfield, St Anne's Vale. She started as a pupil teacher, at St Anne's School, and taught there for over twenty years, until re-organisation took place in 1939. She then moved to Endon Secondary School. She married Mr John Benton, also a teacher at Brown Edge and Endon. After the death of her husband in 1963, Mrs Benton continued to live at Brookfield with two of her sisters, Eunice and Mary. She retired in 1971 and was awarded the MBE for fifty-three years of service to education. She died in 1983. Her experiences were recorded in 1971 and start in the earliest years of the 20th century:

If you were to read in a book about what happened in Brown Edge 60 to 70 years ago, you would have no idea how far back that was, but if I told you that I was a child in this school over 60 years ago, you might get a clearer picture of time. I once asked a class in this school to write what they thought Brown Edge was like 100 years ago and I was astounded to find that they thought people would be running round in skins of animals. I soon explained that my father and grandfather were living 100 years ago and didn't wear skins. 60, 70 or 100 years isn't a very long time but a lot of changes have taken place.

I suppose, really, I should begin to tell you a little of what I remember about my earliest days at school. Today children don't go to school until they are 5, but I went when I was 4 years and 1 month old so I don't remember much about it.

The Infants School was in Church Road, or Lane Ends as we called it, and it is where Merle Harvey now lives. There was no playground, so we were sent into the road to play. There was no supervision but there was not much danger as there were no motor cars. Occasionally a horse and cart could be seen but they moved slowly and we could easily get out of the way.

When I was 6 years old I left the Infants School and came to the Big School. I suppose it was called Big because bigger children attended it. In those days children didn't go to Endon Secondary School when they were 11, but stayed until they were old enough to go to work. As soon as a child's 13th birthday arrived, he would go the headmaster and say 'Please sir, will you look to see if I have made my times?' Then the headmaster would look in the registers to see how many attendances had been made and if the correct number had been made, the child could leave. My parents left school when they were 10.

This school was very much smaller than it is now. The present hall was one classroom containing about four classes and there were two small rooms. The entrance to the school was facing School Bank. In one room was the school bell, pulled by a rope, to ring twice in the morning, once at a quarter to nine and again at 9 o clock. As it was a Church school the Vicar came every morning to open school and every evening to close school.

The children were divided into classes called standards ranging from Standard 0, which contained the backward children, many of whom stayed there until they left school, to Standard 7 or Ex.7.

The rooms were furnished with long desks each holding 4 or 5 children. In these desks were slots in which slates were placed, for most of the written work was done on slates to save the expense of paper. There wasn't much money allowed for education and so paper and books were very scarce. The work on slates was done with slate pencils, which was a piece of slate in the form of a pencil to write down our sums. The teacher came round with a piece of chalk and marked them right or wrong.

While I was at school, slates were banned for health reasons. To clean a slate, you need a duster but this does not fetch off all the marks so children used to spit on the slates and wipe it off with their own duster, but if they hadn't one the boys would use their jacket sleeves and the girls used their pinafores. This of course, was unhygienic, and so slates were banned. When the slate pencils became blunt they were sharpened by rubbing them on a stone window sill and this made grooves in the stone. There is one of these sills showing the grooves in the hall but it has now been painted over.

The slate pencils had another use. There were no school meals provided so the children who lived a distance from the school had to bring sandwiches. The children didn't like this in the cold weather so they used to bring bread and butter sandwiches, take a slate pencil from the cupboard, push it through the bread and toast it in front of a big blazing fire. This was called French toast. There was no supervision by the staff.

There was no water laid on at the school and if we wanted a drink we would take a medicine bottle to Stone House well and fill it with water and drink it. Again there was no supervision although it was an open well.

The lessons at school were very different from what they are today. Every morning for the first lesson we had Scripture or Religious Instruction, the rest of the morning was spent with the 3Rs. For most of the other lessons we had to learn by heart. Our geography lessons consisted of learning the names and locations of capes and bays, tributaries of rivers or the peaks in the mountain ranges, e.g. Flamborough Head and Spurn Head in Yorkshire, Lowestoft ness in Sussex, the Naze in Essex, North Foreland and South Foreland in Kent. or Swale, Ure, Nidd, Wharfe, Aire, Don, Calder (tributaries of the Yorkshire Ouse).

I had a sister much older than I who told me that when she was at school only boys learnt Geography while the girls did Needlework. This was understandable in a way because Needlework was very important to a girl then. Remember there was very little entertainment for people in those days. There was no radio, no television, no cars or buses to take them out of the village, so in the evening the girls spent their time in knitting, darning and sewing. If they wanted new clothes they couldn't jump on a bus and go to Hanley to Marks and Spencers because there were no buses and no Marks and Spencers as such. Even if they possessed a horse and trap, the only clothes they could afford to buy would be badly made or of poor quality so usually the clothes were made at home or by the village dressmaker.

Children in school were not as fortunate as children today. The girls didn't have two or three summer dresses and two or three winter dresses. Because money was very scarce, and there were no family allowances, girls would have one thicker frock in the spring and this would last all the year for best wear, and then be taken for school-wear the next year. It was very necessary to keep these frocks clean because if they were washed they would shrink badly. So every child wore a print pinafore.

The boys wore short trousers, jackets without a collar, and stiff white collars - Eton style. No boy wore long trousers until he went to work.

The girls wore long hair, tied back with a bow of ribbon. Almost all the boys and some of the girls wore clogs because they were cheap, waterproof and durable and were suited for the rough stony roads. The clogs had iron tips renewed by the village clogger.

When the children were ready to leave school, the teachers would know what the children would do. As there were no buses or cars, the work for the boys would have to be within walking distance. It was no good getting a job in Leek or Hanley or Burslem because it would be too far to walk there in the morning and back again at night, so apart from the odd butcher's boy or farm labourer, all the boys went to Whitfield, to work in the coal mine. They came home with black faces because there were no pit baths.

If a girl could not stay at home to keep mother, there was nothing for the girls except domestic service. This meant that a girl would get a job as a domestic servant at a house, perhaps in Endon or Leek, or Burslem and she would live in, coming home perhaps every other Sunday, but even then she had to be back by 9pm. She had to work hard, scrubbing floors, washing or cleaning grates, and for very little wages. There were no washers or vacuum cleaners, or any other labour saving devices.

When the buses came after the First World War all this was changed.

Nearly all the people in the village spoke dialect. In school proper English was spoken but the moment the children were released, dialect was used. Some of the older people couldn't speak English as it is used today. It is only since people have been able to get out of the village that dialect has become less frequently used and although many people still use it, they can also speak correctly.

A presentation to Mr W H Jones. A wallet containing £50 was presented to Mr Jones after 44 years of service as headmaster of the village schools. Mr & Mrs Jones seated, with members of their staff and the committee.
Left to Right: Mr Pointon, Mr L Jones (son), Miss I Weaver, Mrs E Johnson, Mr G Redfern, Mrs G Hall, Miss H Dawson, Miss P Lovatt, Mr Powell, Major Dickinson.

School Garden
Class 1913 with
Walter Jones.

Mrs Jones outside the Schoolmaster's house
looking over the School garden.

A view of the Church and School from Old
Lane. The land in the foreground was sold as
five building plots in 1972.

St Anne's School 1920 class. These are the names Grace Hewitt remembers.
Back row left to right: 1st Edwin Turner, 7th Colin Simcock.
3rd Row L to R: Ada Scarlett, ?, May Berrisford, Grace Dawson, -- Snape, Mabel Turner, Ada Foster, ?, ?.
2nd row L to R: Lottie Grimes, Elsie Wood, Violet Snape, ?, Nelly Chadwick, Florence Slack, Gertie Holford.
Front row L to R: Bill Lomas, Bill Beff, George Henry Stonier, Edward Sherratt, Joe Berrisford, Stephen Bourne.

Infants Top Class, August 1920.   *Back row left to right:* H.Willott, A.Bourne, G.Turner, S.Sheldon, T. Pointon, H. Hughes, W. Cumberlidge.   *Middle Row left to right:* A. Pointon, A. Hodkinson, T. Dawson, A. Hall, W. Hancock, H. J. Bourne, D. Holdcroft, ?.   *Front Row left to right:* C. Sherratt, I. Mountford, C. Weaver, A. Cumberlidge, R. Hargreaves, M Foster, L. Pointon, A. Sheldon.

Honor Dawson with her Class 1920. Arthur Sutton is 7th from the left, back row.

Walter Jones with Classes VI and VII August 1920.
Back Row: H. Lomas, J. Stonier, E. Davenport, A. Frost, A. Pointon, B. Dawson,
F. Berrisford, T. Berrisford, T. Goodwin, F. Slack, C. Lomas, G. Parton, J. Hollins.
Third Row: W. J. Jones, A. Durber, H. Goodwin, A. Simcock, N. Hargreaves, E. Mountford, W. Hargreaves,
P. Goodwin, D. Charlesworth, E. Sherratt, M. Snape A. Lamsdale
2nd Row: A. Foster, I. White, M. Goodwin, E. Chadwick, E. Moss, E. Heath, R. Forrester, D. Knight, A. Simcock, W. Jervis.
Front: W. Hodkinson, G. Dawson, H. Turner, E. Bailey, R. Hancock, S. Gratton, A. Scarlett, F. Dawson, R. Willott, E. Hodkinson

Tom Dawson

I was born at Norton on Easter Monday 1921. My father was Tom Dawson and my mothers name was Florence Edwards, before she was married.

My father was away in Ireland at the time when I was born. He was a soldier in the First World War. He was demobbed in 1918 but as he was a reservist, he was called up when trouble flared up in Ireland. When Dad came home we moved to Silver Street and bought a cottage.

A chap named John Mayer owned some farms up Hough Hill, Brown Edge. My dad had worked for him as a youth and when one of these farms became vacant he asked my dad if he wanted it. He jumped at the chance.

Fernyhough Farm was then two farms, Lower and Upper. We rented Upper and Sam Hargreaves farmed at Lower. Mr Mayer wanted my dad to buy both farms, £1500 for the two, but he hadn't got the money, and folks didn't have mortgages in them days.

I was about seven when I came to Brown Edge. I had a half-sister, Nancy Lowe, who was sixteen. She went off to my Aunt Dolly's at Manchester and trained as a nurse at Manchester Royal, so I didn't see her much.

The farm was about 12$\frac{1}{2}$ acres. Dad also worked in the pit, at Bellerton, as a fireman. When he finished that he worked as a rope maker. We only stayed at Fernyhough for a few years and then we moved to Steinfields, Broad Lane, which was 16 acres. This is what people did - you had one of these places and had a bit of stock, then you went for a bigger place.

When I started at Brown Edge School, at age 7, I went into Class one, Miss Smith's, for a few months. Then I went into Miss Rushton's, Standard 2, for a bit. I then went into Class three, Phyllis Davenport's class. Mr Walter

Tom Dawson aged four in his Sunday best.

Jones was the headmaster and he was very strict. Miss Stonier taught Class four, Mr Benton class 5 and Miss Honor Dawson Class six.

There was a church service to start and end the day, with prayers and hymns learnt by heart. Lessons began with arithmetic and English then history and geography in the afternoon, sometimes with woodwork for the boys and needlework for the girls. There was a lot of parrot fashion learning of tables, names of rivers and dates.

Miss Dawson was also very strict. She only had to point her finger and the room went quiet. Children were always taught respect.

The sports day was popular, with a champion boy and girl. Hilda Beresford was champion a few years, nobody could catch her; she ran like a deer.

We were reasonably well off but Brown Edge was a poor place. There was more folks not working than working. Most children went to school in trousers and jersey and clogs. My mother used to turn me out with a suit and low shoes. Everybody with clogs thought it was their bounden duty to kick my low shoes off.

We did gardening at school. There was a big lawn in front of the headmaster's house, with a weeping willow in the middle. At the far end, close to the Infant's School, was a big rockery, and the garden went right up the field. Mrs Jones was a very nice woman. When we mowed the lawn, if Mr Jones wasn't about, we got a drop of lemonade.

Mr Jones tried to do his best for the village. He ordered all the seeds for the gardeners and allotment holders. He ordered in bulk and got them a lot cheaper. Some of the children had to take a barrow of seeds and deliver them round the village. I was occupied with this.

I was one of those nominated to go in for the scholarship but I nominated myself out of it. I didn't want to go to school in Leek. I wanted to go into farming. There was a bit of to-ing and fro-ing about this and I got belted for it, but I stuck to it. I've always regretted it.

When we were in the second and top class one afternoon a week, we worked in the gardens with Mr Jones. At the top of the garden towards Fosters Row there was going to be a memorial to the First World War dead. Mr Jones and Mr Benton planned it all out and the lads mixed the cement and did the work. There was going to be four big pillars, an archway at the top and a big plinth with the names on. We got to the stage of putting the pillars up and casting the archway when the vicar, Rev. Lawton, came and put a stop to it. It all had to come down. The Vicar was in charge of the school and him and Walter Jones didn't always get on. But he let us get started and then stopped it.

Boys at school working on the World War 1 memorial, which later had to be taken down.

The real boss was the rector from Norton. He came twice a year to look round. He was the real 'bees knees'. He wore breeches, and waistcoat, all in black, and buttoned gaiters.

I left school when I was 14. My dad still worked in the pit. At Steinfields we had 8 cows, a horse, 3 or 4 stirks and 50 or 60 hens and we all helped.

The day I left school, it was the day before Good Friday and we had only just moved to Steinfields. My mother wanted to go to my Auntie Annie's at Derby. She fixed up to go with my Auntie Dolly, for the weekend, but she never came home. She died when she was there. She was only 42, it was a cerebral haemorrhage. My mother was a big strapping woman, nobody could believe she was dead. She always went like the clappers. She'd never had anything to do with farming, she'd been a mill worker at Leek, but she'd settled into it.

It's no good on a farm without a woman. When my mother died my dad was totally lost. We had a housekeeper for a while called Jesse. She was very good but it's not the same. So Dad gave up the farm after just two years. The times were bad for small farmers.

Eventually Dad got in with a Mrs Hancock from Lane Ends and married her, I was 16 then. We went to live at Lane Ends in her bungalow, where John Holdcroft lives now. She was a very, very good stepmother. I was working in the pit then.

One day Dad and my stepmother went to Burslem to get a new suit. He collapsed in the tailors and they had to get him a taxi home. It was a heart attack. He died 8 or 9 months later. He was 42 and had always looked as fit as a fiddle.

I carried on living with my stepmother and she lived with us after I was married, 27 years altogether. She was very good to us.

I was working at Whitfield and very often walked there and rode back on Turner's bus. It was nothing to walk down the fields to Tongue Lane, most of the men on Brown Edge walked that way. If you were on noons and had to stop over a bit, you'd miss the bus and it was a bit scary walking up in the dark. There was a war on, you either liked it or lumped it. You couldn't leave the pit, there was nowhere to go.

When I was eighteen I started courting. Her name was Lily Jervis and she was sixteen. She lived near to me, at Rose Cottage. We used to go to the Band Room on Saturday nights. This was on High Lane, opposite the Sytch, and it used to get packed to the doors!! The sides went in and out! They used to come from everywhere to the Band Room: Baddeley Green, Endon, Ball Green and Biddulph Moor. The place used to be rocking. Arthur Sherratt used to run it and he played the piano. Herbert Sherratt played the drums, May and Rene piano accordion and George Lilley played the fiddle. There was never any bother or fighting. At a quarter to twelve it closed down, everybody filed out. You could have heard a pin drop down Sandy Lane.

In those days nobody had got much money for drink. When you left school you had about 2/6p week pocket money. Beer was 5 pence a pint, you could afford a couple at the most! There was the Hollybush, Roe Buck and Lump of Coal on the main road. The Colliers Arms up Hough Hill was more middle-age trade.

When I was about 27 I had an accident in the pit. The roof caved in and I never thought I'd come out. It was a bad place: two men were setting extra timber and I told them to go and get their snappin. I was just looking at it and it came down. I thought what am I going to do now, I couldn't move a finger. I thought they'll never be able to get through to me, there's nothing I can do about it. I was trapped for six hours. After a long time trapped I heard a spade push into the dirt and I thought, 'Someone knows I'm here'. I heard someone say 'I can feel his hat'. They were scratching at the top of my helmet.

They thought it was just a matter of lifting me out, except my legs were fast between two girders. They nearly pulled me in two trying to pull me out. They had to clear all around to get to my legs but the dirt kept running down. They had to keep clearing it and put wood to hold it back. The doctor came on the job and he'd have had both legs off before you could bat your eye. By this time I was so fed up I didn't care what they did. They could have nipped them off at my waist if they'd wanted.

A big man from Chell Heath, Cyril Dodd, said 'Hang on a bit before you start cutting any legs off, let me have a do at this'. There was a chap named Tommy Wilkinson, he'd got his arm fastened, and until they got him out they couldn't get to me. He had to pull his arm out and I had to watch his flesh curl up on his arm as they pulled him.

Then Cyril Dodd got his arm right through the girders, got a jack knife and cut my boots off. He then got hold of the outside of my foot, turned it over and he managed to sneak it out. The men then turned me over completely to get me out. It was hair-raising I'll tell you.

By the time they got me out, the Manager had lined teams of men all the way up from the Bullhurst to the pit bottom. They put me on a stretcher and four blokes ran out to the next four and so on. I must have got to the pit bottom in record time.

I went up in the cage and they ran with me to the ambulance and off to hospital. When I got there they put me in bed just as I was, as black as club ten.

After a while there was a woman standing looking at me, she said 'Are you awake? Are you the chap who was brought in last night who's been buried? Have you had any breakfast? I'll see you get some'. She came back later and said 'I'm sorry it was too late, they've only got kippers'. My hands were like boxing gloves so I said 'I'm sorry that's no good'. She wandered off, her part done. Later when I was waiting on the trolley a woman came and gave me half of a half pound block of chocolate and I chewed on that.

They said there was nothing broken, I was badly bruised and knocked everywhere but they said I could go home. They never did wash me, I went home as I was. I was on crutches for a week or two and had no feeling in my feet. At least I had both my legs.

When Lily and I were married we carried on living in the bungalow, at Lane Ends, with my stepmother. One night I sat talking to Joe Cumberlidge on the wall outside his shop. He told me that the Free Mission, at Hill Top, was closing. At the time you could not get a bit of land in Brown Edge for love nor money. I went to see Jack Charlesworth and asked him if he would sell it to me. He said, if we could agree a price, it was mine.

It was a brick building and I had a vision of just putting a few windows in. When I came to look, it had no foundations in. I took it down a bit at a time, put foundations in, cleaned the bricks and rebuilt it. I got some old books from the library. I couldn't get a mortgage because I was building it myself. We also had to buy the land at the back for a garden. It took me four years to build. I worked on it after work and at weekends. We have been here now for about 40 years.

Florence Dawson, Tom's Mum.

Tom Dawson Senior, in uniform.

Tom Dawson Senior at Steinfields.

Lily Jervis, Tom's wife.

Lily's grandmother, Annie Turner, outside her cottage
in Sandy Lane.

Lily's other Grandparents, George and Lizzie Jervis.
They lived at Rose Cottage, Church Road. George
was known as 'Old Jarve' and was a big gardener.

Dick Turner. Lily's Grandad.

Tom on the left, with Trevor Worsley.
Tom was showing Trevor round Norton Pit.

Miners' Convalescent Home at Rudyard. Tom Dawson senior is on the back row 4th from the right.

First World War soldiers. Tom Dawson senior is 4th from the left, back row.

First World War group. Tom Dawson senior is 3rd from the left, second row.

Many Brown Edge men worked as miners mainly at Norton and Chatterley Whitfield Collieries. Miners are seen here at Norton Colliery c.1900. Charles Hargreaves is fourth from the right.

THE RESCUE TEAM FROM WHITFIELD COLLIERY.
Alan Pointon is on the left carrying a caged canary. This team assisted at the Sneyd Pit disaster, 1st January 1942.

Philip Durber

My grandfather, John William Proctor, went into farm service at the age of nine, but he got the sack. He then went into the Pit and worked there until he was sixty-five. He never learnt to read or write but he must have been a good, practical collier because he finished up as a Senior Overman at Bellerton Colliery.

He used to live in a cottage in High Lane when he was first married, then he went to St Anne's Vale. He later moved to Hodgefields, where he kept some cows. He walked to Bellerton and back every day. A lot of miners at this time had a bit of a smallholding.

He then moved to High Lane Farm and this is where he stayed. He had eleven children and my mother, Pattie, was the eldest girl. When she was thirteen and leaving school, the rector came and asked her mother if she could stay on and be a teacher. My grandmother said no, because she was needed at home. She said she would consider it for Kate, the next eldest. Out of eleven children four of them became schoolteachers.

I think my grandad Proctor was a remarkable man. He was a very hard worker and a fair man, but my mother said he was bad-tempered. He used to farm with my Uncle Frank and they owned about twenty acres down High Lane. He bought two houses opposite and also had two houses built. Even although he owned four houses, he still rented High Lane Farm.

My grandmother used to go to Miss Heaton's at Poolfield House for a Sunday afternoon ladies' class. She always said she could be good if she lived somewhere like that. Her name was Hannah Simcock and she came from Old Lane, before she was married.

I was born in 1925 at Knypersley Mill Farm. My father, William Durber, used to live at Ladymoorgate Farm. When he married my mother, Pattie Proctor, they first lived at Yew Tree Farm, Norton Green. My mother used to say they never left their shoes on the floor at night because of the cockroaches.

Dad bought Mill Farm at the sale in 1919, but didn't actually move in until about 1920.

Philip's dad, William Durber, at Mill Farm, Knypersley Pool c.1937.

Arthur Durber, Harvey Durber's father was there before us. We had a thriving corn business and also milked about twenty cows. Jim Holdcroft used to help us.

I was the only surviving child. My mother lost a son, John Proctor Durber, in about 1922, and also a girl, who died in infancy. Mother was determined that I was to be educated. She sent me to Brown Edge Infant's School but Miss Garner, the headmistress, sent me home with a letter saying that I was too young. So that was that.

I was getting down to the mill a lot and I think I was extending my vocabulary along dodgy lines. A girl named Edith Handley, who lived at Ridgeway Hall Farm, was going to Miss Heaton's, a private school, and mother decided that was where I was going to go.

Miss Heaton's school was at Poolfield House, Brown Edge. Miss Kate ran it and another sister Lydia, kept house. There were about fourteen of us, mostly girls. There was only another lad there, besides me, and I didn't like it. As far as I remember we just did religious education, English and arithmetic. I was there about three years but I got that I didn't want to go. When I was about seven I went to Brown Edge School. I was in Miss Rushton's class, Miss Davenport's, Miss Stonier's and finished up in Mr Benton's class.

I left when I was nearly eleven. I took the scholarship and went to Wolstanton Grammar School. Walter Jones, the headmaster at Brown Edge, is thought of as a gardener because of the big school garden he had, and he also ran the sports - Sports Day was big in Brown Edge. However, looking back, I think that the main thing was that he believed children, who had the ability, should be given the chance to go to High School. He would send three or four pupils to Leek each year. In the big room in school there was a board up with scholarship names on.

I was the first one to go to Wolstanton. I used to have to walk to Black Bull to catch a bus. It was a long day for me. I didn't come out of school until 4:30pm and if I was lucky I caught a Well's bus at a quarter to five, and then had to walk from Black Bull. A Brown Edge lad worked at the station and, if I was there before he knocked off, he used to give me a ride on his bike, on the crossbar. We used to come down Greenway Bank like mad but I never fell off.

When we were at Knypersley Mill Farm I used to milk my share of the cows, alongside Jim Holdcroft and my dad. I had the easy ones. I was a good milker, I wanted to do it. I never did any once I was going to Wolstanton though. My mother was a strong woman, very good, but she laid the law down and education came first.

As there were a lot of families in Brown Edge with the same surname, nicknames were used. I remember there used to be a cobbler, named Sheldon, who lived behind Harvey's Mission at Hill Top. He worked in a shed there. Dad said one day 'Take these shoes to Numpys'. I went up there, knocked on his shed door and said 'Morning Mr Numpy'. He wasn't very pleased.

One day my dad went with John Holdcroft to Newcastle Market. They'd taken a big old boar to sell, in a large pig crate. At the end of the sale Dad bought a pony, for three quarters of a guinea, which was fifteen shillings and nine pence. It had never been ridden. We

Philip, by the Millhouse, on his pony 1934.

broke it in and it taught us how to ride, by falling off! I was about seven. I called it Doll and went everywhere on it.

My father died when I was twelve and we left the farm and went to live in Ball Lane. When I was seventeen, nearly eighteen, I went to Durham University. I had my mother to thank for my education and also Walter Jones. The head of Wolstanton, Mr Marples, also believed that children of working class parents, should, if they had the ability, go to university.

I did a year at university and then the army beckoned. Well I thought it was but I was one of the Bevin Boys drawn out of a hat. When you were called up (registered for National Service) you were given a registration number (of 5 or 6 digits), for example 345210. Mr Ernest Bevin, the Minister of Labour, had a tombola arrangement with ten numbers in (0 to 9). The numbers were given a good shake and then Mr Bevin pulled out one number, in this case 0. All those young men, whose registration number ended with 0, were directed to the mines.

On the 5th November 1944, I received notification that for my national service I was to report to Kemball Pit Training Centre on the 13th November and the wages would be £3 per week. Thus I became a Bevin Boy. After a month's training, 10 days practical at Kemball Pit and 10 days theory at Tunstall mining school, I arrived at Chatterley Whitfield Colliery.

After another short introductory course on the surface, I descended the middle pit shaft and can remember standing at the top of the Hardmine Dip on that first morning. It was all so confusing and rather frightening – men shouting, joking, laughing, trolleys being thrown over - I thought I'd never get used to this - but I did.

The first six months or so were spent working on the haulage around the pit bottom area with three other Brown Edge lads - Fred Willott, Sam Slack and Frank Fox. The rest of my first year was spent working with four elderly gentlemen, Bill James, Sam Cartlidge, Sam Slack (father) and Straub (I cannot remember his real name) in the Little Row District, which at the time was a development area. The job was of a roving kind and my mentor Bill James was very good with me, always showing me how to do different tasks. How I came to be working with such an elderly experienced team I do not know, but of course it did not last.

At the start of 1946 the newly constructed Bellringer face in the Little Row District started to produce coal and I found myself working as a haulage hand on the Little Row turn (days and noons).

The following August on the recommendation of Mr Wilcox (the manager) I moved to the laboratory (9am - 4.30pm) - much better than those 6am starts. My duties included collecting air and dust samples from all those pits, Hesketh, Institute and Middle, and the analysis of those samples on the surface. Demobilisation came in December 1947, so I said goodbye to Chatterley Whitfield and went back to university. I did return to Chatterley Whitfield, in the Summer holidays, when they found a job for me in the laboratory.

I first met my wife, Olwyn Lear, in 1943 when I was eighteen and she was sixteen. It was at a 'Dig for Victory' dance, held at Norton Green School. We were married on 1st January 1955. I bought some land off my Uncle Frank and we had a house built in High Lane, which we still live in. We have had two daughters and they are both teachers.

When I was about twenty-five I went back to Wolstanton as a physics teacher. It was my mother's doing again. She sent me the advert and I applied and got the job. I stayed for twelve years. Mr Marples, the head, left in 1961 and I felt I was getting to be part of the furniture. I left and got a job at Oakhill for six years. I then came to Endon Secondary School as deputy

A loaded pony at Mill farm 1936. *L to R* Janet Proctor, Mary Proctor, Flo Clowes, David Clowes, Rosemary Hargreaves, Philip, John Proctor, Pattie Durber (Mum).

head to Mr Hawley. I had never lived in my own catchment area before. I later became the headmaster at Endon, which I did for fifteen years, until my retirement.

When Brown Edge became a council of its own, in 1965, I became a parish councillor. After Jack Rushton's retirement I stood in his place as District Councillor,

which I did for twelve years.

I have always attended St Anne's Church and been involved with the fetes and money raising activities. John Fenton was an incredible man. He always did a lot for the Church and we worked on the churchyard together. I think the first queen's garden party was held at Rock Cottage with Janet Proctor as queen. My uncle, Harry Proctor, used to run the garden parties. It is good that they still continue today,

Philip in his office, at Endon High School, on his last day of office as Headmaster

A family break at Blackpool, 1963. Philip and Olwyn with their daughters Celia, on the right and Jean on the left.

The Proctor sisters outside Sunnyside, High Lane 1937.
Back Row L-R: Gladys, Flo, Eva. *Front Row L-R:* Grace, Effie, Kate, Pattie.

The Proctor family outside High Lane Farm. *Back Row left to right:* Eva, Effie, Pattie, Harry, Kate, Grace, Frank.
Front Row L-R: John William, Flo, Gladys, Bob, Hannah. A son William is not pictured as he emigrated to Australia.

Grandma and Grandad at their Golden
Wedding 1933.
Hannah and John William Proctor.

Gladys Proctor's Wedding in the early 1930s
Left to right: Eva, ?, Eric Hargreaves,
Gladys, Bob, Flo. This is taken in front of
High Lane Farm.

Laboratory workers at Walsall Wood Colliery, 1947. This was when Philip was a 'Bevin Boy' - he is
the tall one wearing his cap the Brown Edge way.

Wolstanton Grammar School – a GCE exam has just started.
Philip is in charge and the headmaster Mr Marples is in the background.

Betty Hargreaves nee Lowe

I'm 104 in March. I was born in 1902 at Hill Top, in a house in Broad Lane. It's still there. My mother was Sarah Ellen Rigby and she came from Chesterton. My father, James Lowe, was born in Brown Edge, in a house at the top of Hough Hill, near the Free Mission. We used to go to the Mission twice every Sunday.

My mother's mother died very young. She was having another baby and slipped on a cockroach on the stairs. She died, and the baby too. Mother's stepmother wasn't very good to them, she hit them with sticks. Mother got a train to Endon, she had got a job cleaning at The Plough. They said a gentleman would meet her, with a pony and trap, to bring her to the pub. The man was my father and that's how they met. Mother lived in at The Plough.

When they were married they lived at Hill Top. Dad worked at Black Bull Colliery. They had three children, Enoch, Lottie and Annie, who all died before I was born. Then there was Bob, Mary, Ginnie, me, Jack then Nellie. Nellie died too. My mother was a wonderful mother but my father had a lot to drink. I didn't like my father. We only saw him at weekends. He had to walk to work, and went out before we were up. We were in bed when he got home.

We had no water in the house. We had to fetch water from Star Well or Lane Well, Hill Top, before and after school. We had a tank at the back of the house to catch rain water. We used to have a bath in front of the fire. We had a wooden bath, then later a tin one, and all bathed in the same water. We had a dog, called Monty, and he had the last wash. Mother and Father must have had theirs when we were in bed. They didn't wash like we wash today, you know.

For breakfast mother used to have dripping toast and beer warmed over the fire. Tea was too expensive then, we used to buy it in 2 ounces. We were very poor but mother always found something for us to eat. On a Friday she hadn't got two halfpennies to rub together, until my father came home. She used to cook some ends of bacon, a few potatoes, boiled with Oxo, and a bit of bread. It was tasty.

We had a little garden there and some fowl. Mum used to make all her own jams. We loved my mother but I didn't love my father. We had a pig of our own and would kill it, put plenty of salt on it and hang it in the kitchen. At Christmas we would have some pork and a big pudding with currants in.

Father's brother, Uncle George, owned three little cottages opposite the pub at Hill top. I think I was about seven or eight when we went to live in the middle one. Uncle George lived in one and another auntie lived in the third one.

I went to school, at five, to Lane Ends Infant School. I didn't like school. My sisters used to take me and I used to hit and kick them. I was a naughty girl. I liked history and geography though. At playtime I used to run off and go up Marshes Hill, at bilberry time. I wore navy knickers, with a pocket in, and used to keep an empty sugar bag in it, to put the fruit in. They used to keep me in at playtime to stop me going up Marshes Hill. Mother never hit me, she just said I was a naughty girl.

Billy Jones, the Master, was Welsh and had a lot to drink. He fell over a wall at Lane Ends once, and got a black eye. He used to give you a slap up the side of the face if you got anything wrong. Another teacher, Walter Jones, used to make you do exercises, made you bend and twist, and I didn't like that. We went to school in clogs and made our own pinafores to wear.

I left school at thirteen and went to work for a family of nine at Mill Hayes Road,

Biddulph. I walked there in my clogs, carrying a tin box with a morning and afternoon frock in, and an apron. I don't know where the box is now. My mother said knock on the door and say 'I've come to see if I'll do'. Their name was Goode and they lived at the top of the bank, on the right, near Knypersley Farm. Mr Goode was a manager at Black Bull. I was the only servant and I had to do everything.

The first job was to clean all the brass knockers on the doors and light fires. I got up at 6 o'clock and went to bed about ten or eleven o'clock. I did all the washing up, cleaning, scrubbing yards and windows, inside and out. It was hard work, they don't know they're born today. It was like prison. I had a half day off on Wednesdays and every other Sunday, and got half a crown a week.

I lived in the kitchen on my own. I had a scrubbed top table, a chair and a sofa, but I hadn't much time for sitting down. I wore a print dress in the morning and a black dress, white cap and apron for the afternoon. It was to make sure you weren't one of them, all a lot of rubbish wasn't it?

The eldest daughter, Winifred, married the vicar from Brown Edge, Rev. Page. One of the daughters did the cooking and made all the bread. I was there for nearly thirteen years. I got browned off and fed up with it.

I got a new job in Tunstall, opposite the park. He was a solicitor called Dodds and they had nine children, but four or five of them were away at school. They later moved to Endon, a big house called Woodside, down Clay Lake. I was cook, house parlour maid and nurse. They also had a kitchen maid. My sister, at Brown Edge, used to come Monday to do the washing and she came Tuesdays to help me polish the dining room floor. She's dead now, they all are. I'm the last one. It was a big house with three lots of stairs. I bet it's altered now you know. They had a big garden, orchards and a field with a donkey.

I stayed there until I got married, when I was thirty five. They were very nice, I shouldn't have stuck it that long else.

Mr Dodds went to London once a month and I used to pack his case for him and he gave me five pounds for doing that. Mrs Dodds used to say 'Betty I should save that, put it in the bank. If you get married don't tell your husband, it's your money'.

Betty with her niece and namesake, Betty Lowe. This was taken at Ridgway c.1930.

I used to do a meal for 7 o'clock. I used to do pork, beef or pheasant. The gardener used to pluck the pheasants. Their favourite pudding was lemon meringue pie. When they had visitors, for a meal, I went round with a serviette on my arm and a little bottle. When they'd finished their dinners they used to put their fingers in and wash them and dry them on this towel. All that fuss and bother.

On holiday at Blackpool, with Mrs Dodds, I had my fortune told. She said 'You haven't got a young man but you're going to have one', and she told me I'd be going down a lane and he'd be leaning over a wall. He'll have dark black hair. It all happened. It was Enoch Hargreaves from Spout House. I had been to visit my sister at Brown Edge and he said 'Shall I walk down with you', and I said, 'Ooh Yes'.

When I told Mrs Dodds I wanted to get married she said 'I want to see your young man'. He had to go in the lounge and have a drink. She said 'I think he'll be alright!' They were very good when I left to get married. I didn't have to buy a crock, kitchenware, tea and supper ware, blankets or bed covers. They rigged me up with everything. A sideboard, table and chairs were the only things we bought.

Grandma Hargreaves, from Spout House, gave us our house when we got married. It was Avonglen, now called The Granary in St Anne's Vale. My husband worked at Bellerton but then he went into the building trade. He worked for Frost in Brown Edge. They're all dead now. Our house was very small with stone stairs but my husband did a lot of work on it. He put on another bedroom, kitchen, bathroom and a new yard.

A view of The Vale taken by Mr Charles in 1953. The house facing on the left is where Aunt Martha lived. Avonglen is at the side of Aunt Martha's and it is where Betty lived when she got married.

Left: Betty in the garden at Avonglen.

I had five children but lost two little girls, Anne and Nellie. David is the oldest, then Nona and Sheila. Dr Glass brought David into the world. He was only a seven month baby. He was wrapped in cotton wool and olive oil for five months. I looked after him and had him downstairs. He had milk from Spout House, from one special cow, and I put glucose in it. I never saw a doctor until I had our David. My father was

A surprise party for Betty on her 70th Birthday, at the Unicorn, Leek.
Betty's two sisters, Ginnie and Mary are each side of her. Betty is holding Anita.

ninety-two when he died, in his sleep. I'd never known my father have a cold, or cough or be off sick or anything. He'd never seen a doctor, never had any teeth out, glasses or anything. He was never poorly. Mother died in her eighties.

I used to work a bit at Heatons at Poolfields House. I did a bit of charring when I was married. Three sisters lived there and a brother. He walked to Burslem every day, where he worked. The youngest sister went out shopping every day. She always bought a lot of bananas. They never ought to have taken that house down and put a club there. It was a beautiful house, plenty of ground to it, and under the wall, daffodils used to come up. They all died, one after the other.

Mrs Baddeley had a little shop on the village. She used to sell paraffin and sticks and we always used to knock the sticks to make the cockroaches come out. We used to have a lot of cockroaches at Brown Edge at one time.

I got a job at Moorlands Hospital, in Leek, when I was fifty nine, cleaning, cooking and everything. I worked there until I was seventy-three, when a new matron finished four of us.

I am the oldest customer the Co-op has got. I joined at thirty-five and go every Thursday, to Leek. They take me in the wheelchair from the Day Centre. On my birthday they got me a bottle of wine, some flowers and a box of chocolates. They have a big fuss at the centre for me too.

My sister, Ginnie Willott, died at Norton Green Nursing Home, when she was 102 . I want to die here, in my own home. My eyes are very bad but I still knit. I knit squares for blankets and take them to the Centre. I can put stitches on, but if I drop a stitch I have to unrove the lot and start again. I manage somehow. If I didn't do that, I'd go barmy cause I can't see to do anything else. I've always managed to get a living. I don't owe a penny to anybody, everything's paid for.

Betty's recipe for longevity: *Clean living, no pubs, no smoking, have beef dripping, plain eating. That's the recipe, and hard work never kills anybody, just the thought of it.*

Betty Celebrating her 100th Birthday.

Annie Shallcross nee Cumberlidge

I was born in 1914, in St Anne's Vale, in a house opposite to where Mrs Benton lived. It was

a house that my Uncle George Hargreaves had built. When I was six my uncle wanted to sell the house but Dad could not afford it. Instead he bought a house at Hill Top and I have lived there ever since. It cost £500. Dad's name was Joseph Cumberlidge.

I had an older brother called Bob and a brother called Joe, six years younger than me. My mother's name, before she was married, was Grace Sheldon and she was born at the Lump of Coal at Brown Edge. Her father, Richard Sheldon, kept the pub for 47 years.

Annie with her brothers, Bob on the left and Joe in the middle.

The Lump of Coal used to be a row of thatched stone cottages. A date inside says 1610. My grandfather put on another storey, doing all the work himself. My grandmother said she carried the bricks for him up the ladder but she wouldn't do it again. She used to say 'Don't do as I've done, do as I say!'

My grandfather also built two cottages across the road from the pub. He also did carpentry and made presents for all the children. Their other children were, as I remember, Rachel, Annie, Harriet, Sam, Tom and George.

Grandfather's brother, Tom, kept a butchers shop next to the pub. This was later Johnson's grocery shop. Aunt Harriet also ran the butchers shop and they sold almanacs as well. She used to sing little songs to us, she was very funny.

I remember my grandparents had someone living with them called Milly. I think they adopted her; she'd just been left somewhere.

My grandfather Richard 'Dick' Sheldon died in 1929, aged 90. He was always very active doing his own property repairs, up to a few days before he died. Uncle George took over the pub in 1909. Locals used to call it 'Cob-o-Slack'.

My father's parents were Joseph and Sarah Cumberlidge and they came from Meerbrook. They lived on a farm but it was flooded when they made Tittesworth Reservoir.

Dad worked at Whitfield. I was close to my Mum. We used to sit at her feet and she would tell us funny stories. I was a bit frightened of my Dad. He was a good man but was the opposite of Mum.

I have always been a member of St Anne's Church. As soon as I could walk I had to go. The two Miss Heatons from Poolfields House used to collect me and walk me along. They were two big ladies with walking sticks and I was frightened to death of them.

When I went to St Anne's School Mr Walter Jones was the head. He was very strict. If you went to church and Mr Jones was in, my goodness you didn't dare speak. I was friends with his niece, Annie Mould, and when I went to her home, if Mr Jones was there I always stood up. He used to say to me 'Don't stand up, you're not in school now'.

Grandfather Joseph Cumberlidge.

Grandmother Sarah Cumberlidge.

Grandfather Richard Sheldon.

Grandmother Harriet Sheldon.

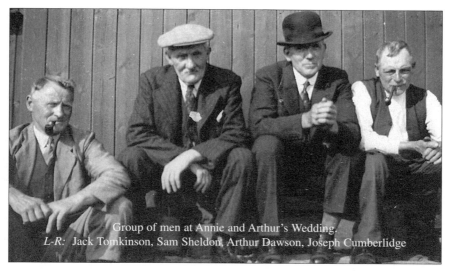

Group of men at Annie and Arthur's Wedding.
L-R: Jack Tomkinson, Sam Sheldon, Arthur Dawson, Joseph Cumberlidge

My brother Bob hated school, he was very stubborn and wouldn't go. He had the cane. We were frightened to death of it, but now they don't care two hoots.

I also used to go to Sunday School in Church House. The vicar's daughter, Miss Mary Lawton, used to take it.

I left school at 14 and went to work at Premier, Buxton Road, Leek. I was on packing, they had lots of different materials there on big rolls. I used to walk to Endon to catch the bus to Leek. I had a friend, Alice Bamford, and I used to go to her house at dinnertime. We are still in touch. She lived up Buxton Road.

My mother was taken ill and I had to stay at home to look after her, my dad and my brothers. I was courting then with Arthur Shallcross. He lived at Mow Cop and used to come over on his bike. We first met at Knypersley Pool.

Mother died in 1939 when I was 25. She was only 56. Arthur and I were married the following year at Brown Edge Church. It was a low-key affair, held at the house afterwards, as it had only been twelve months since Mother died. Dad wouldn't come to the wedding, he said it was too soon.

So Arthur and I lived with Dad and my brothers at Hill Top. Dad died in 1951 of a heart attack, and as Bob and Joe had got married it meant Arthur and I were alone for the first time since our wedding.

Arthur worked as a lorry driver at the Pit. He used to go all over, delivering coal to Lancashire to the big cotton mills. My brother Joe had a grocery shop in Church Road, opposite the churchyard. It's been knocked down now. He also had a catering business and I helped him, waiting on. My brother

Annie with her mum Grace Cumberlidge nee Sheldon.

Annie's Uncle Sam Sheldon, on the left, with his brother Jack and the dog. The cottage is opposite Steinfields, in Broad Lane.

Annie with Arthur.

Annie, on her bike, and Arthur Shallcross before they were married, c.1934.

Arthur and Annie's Wedding in 1940, taken next to the chapel in Chapel Lane.

Nativity in St Anne's Church with Annie as Mary and Vera Cumberlidge as Joseph.
Also pictured are Alice Proctor, Edith Stonier, Annie Mitchell, Gladys Hammond, Florrie Hancock,
Joan Berrisford, Dorothy Bourne.

Bob used to work on Turner's buses.

There was a teacher at the school called Mrs Joy who lived at Stockton Brook. I used to do some cleaning for her. I remember walking down, with my daughter Irene, in the holidays. I did the cleaning, then Mrs Joy gave us some lunch and we walked back. I got 5 shillings.

As we had no transport all our entertainment was on the village. We were always dressing up. The church had a drama group and all the family were involved. Mrs Bond and Mrs Wright started it up with Rev. Attoe. We practiced once a week and did all our own lighting and sets. It was held in the school and was always well supported.

We were always going on trips, with the bell-ringers or choir, and the men had their own outings as well. We always had a big Harvest Supper and all the women made home-made pies. Philip Durber used to auction everything off. I have always enjoyed the Church Fetes. Until quite recently I always helped with the refreshments, making a loaf of sandwiches and baking some cakes.

There is still a Women's Institute but the Mother's Union finished about 2 years ago. I had been a member a long while, and my mother before me.

Later I worked as a dinner lady at St Anne's School with Annie Willott and Elsie Charlesworth. It was hard work because we had to lift down big wooden tables and stack them afterwards. The dinners were brought in then. I retired in 1976 and they presented me with £20, which seemed a lot of money.

I still live at Hill Top where I have lived since I was six. I still get out a lot and go to church, the over 60s and the Fellowship in Hill Top Chapel. I go out for lunch whenever I can and some trips. I have lost a lot of my family and friends over the years but I still get a lot of visitors. I still bake cakes and make jam and keep myself busy.

Annie's retirement from school 1976. *L-R:* Rev. Moseley, Annie, Harry Hammond, Joy Tatton, ?, Mrs Hurst, Evelyn Forrester, ?, Gladys Bailey, Mrs Johnson, Phyllis Huxley, Audrey Holdcroft.

Kitty Clowes nee Boulton

I was born in 1921 at Spout House, Brown Edge and have lived here all my life; four generations of my family have lived here. My father, George Boulton, came from Baddeley Edge. He used to live in a house there, also called Spout House, in Spout Lane.

My mothers' name, before she was married, was Charlotte Hargreaves and her mother's maiden name was Anne Proctor. My dad was a market gardener. He worked at Matthews in Stockton Brook. He loved gardening and was still doing it when he was ninety. He died at the age of ninety-five. My mother died when she was eighty-eight. Her father was Charles Hargreaves.

This used to be a smallholding and I lived here with my mother and father and my grandma and grandad Hargreaves. I was an only child. We farmed about six acres and had cows, pigs, calves and hens. The pigs were fattened up and slaughtered at the place across the

Kitty at Spout House c.1927.

road, now converted into a house. We milked the cows in the shed and delivered the milk.

I remember we used to take milk to Poolfields House where the two Heaton sisters kept a boarding school. It was a lovely house. It's gone now. They also had a brother, called Richard, and a housekeeper called Mrs Newton.

We had no mains water but we were fortunate in having Spout Well at the bottom of the garden. When we did have mains water I could always tell the difference. They used to test me with a glass of each. The spring water was always cold and it was so soft we never needed to use much soap.

My mother made all her own bread and also all the butter. It was a butter churn without a handle, one you had to keep pushing up and down. I used to get fed up and say to my mother 'Is it finished yet?' and she used to say, 'No, you'll have to keep on a bit longer.' I loved buttermilk, I used to drink gallons of it, and it was beautiful. I used to take a can of it when we were haymaking.

My dad also kept two horses and had a governor's cart. We had about forty turkeys every year to fatten up for Christmas. We plucked them all in the house. Dad sold them to Boyce Adams in Hanley and Harrison's Butchers, Brown Edge.

I used to go to Brown Edge School. I remember Mrs Williams and Miss Stonier, John Benton and Honor Dawson; Mr Walter Jones was the Head. I loved icing Christmas cakes with Miss Dawson and also doing needlework. Mr Benton took music.

I remember doing skipping at school, rounders and playing tiddlywinks with buttons. I used to love dressing up when it was Sports Day. I remember once going as bride and groom, half of me dressed as the bride and the other the groom. We used to walk round the village.

I left school at fourteen and went to work at Hammersley's in Burslem. It was a haberdashery shop. I also worked at Woolworths in Leek.

We had a chapel next door to us but I always went up to Hill Top Chapel; my grandad always went there. I remember going to camp meetings on Marshes Hill. We always used to find a big hole to sit in. It was a lovely service, I really enjoyed it.

There was also a 'Bright Hour' in the little old chapel in Sandy Lane which I went to. It had a pot stove in the middle of the room. Sometimes I used to listen outside so I could tell my grandma what they'd been doing, then I used to sneak off 'ladding' instead.

I used to love dance music, I still have to tap my feet now, but I was not allowed to go to the Band Room. We were not allowed to go dancing, it was not decent and we would get up to no good. There was never any trouble there. I used to stand outside listening to the music whenever I could.

Sandy Lane has changed a lot. The Chapel has been taken down. There used to be Mrs Berrisford's

Kitty's dad George Boulton.

chip shop and Harrison's butchers. Mrs Crossley used to sell home-made cakes, then she went to where the paper shop is now. Lily Dawson and her mother had a general store. We used to go to the old Co-op which was later a printing shop, opposite Heaton Villas. Mr Dutton was the manager and we used to get our corn from there for the hens.

During the war, as a lot of the men were away, I got a job at Co-op dairies in Sneyd Green. I used to deliver milk, in a horse and dray, to Sandyford and Goldenhill area. It was hard work but you got more money if you drove. I remember, in the frosty weather, I had chilblains on my hands. At the end of the day I had to brush the horse down. I remember once the horse bolted when we were at traffic lights in Burslem, they were on red. I just closed my eyes; I didn't want to see where I landed. Fortunately I was alright.

On Sundays when there were no buses I used to have to walk to Sneyd Green. Sometimes my dad would walk with me as far as Smallthorne, as he was worried about me, on dark mornings.

I used to get to know people on my rounds and one lady used to make her own oatcakes and she used to give me a breakfast. One day when I knocked at the door of one of my regulars, it was answered by a soldier, in uniform. It was the lady's son and my future husband. He asked me out for a date and that was that.

We married at Brown Edge Church on 30th December 1944. My husband, Edgar Clowes, was on compassionate leave at the time as he had war injuries. He had to return to war service shortly after the wedding.

After the war Edgar returned to his old job as a polisher at Grindy's, a pottery at Tunstall. He came to live at Spout House with me and my parents.

I remember Mrs Powditch first asked me to come along to the W.I. We had lots of fun in those days. I enjoyed dressing up and being in the pantomimes and shows, I still like to go on outings.

I love Brown Edge and wouldn't live anywhere else.

Kitty in Sunday Best for studio photo c.1931.

Kitty and school friends.
Front row L to R: Alice Durber, Ida Beardmore, Joan Ellis, --Bailey, -- Hughes, Frances Biddulph.
Second row L to R: Winnie Dawson, -Rogers, Kitty Boulton, Eileen Pointon, Nelly Foster.
Back row L to R: Marjorie Roberts, Gladys Whitehouse, Joan Bartlem, Maude Snape, Margaret Hopwood, Elsie Beff.

Kitty and Edgar's wedding in 1944.
Left to right: Mary Bowyer, Cyril Clowes, Alma
Proctor, Edgar, Kitty, ?, George Boulton, ?.

W.I. Black and White Minstrels.
Back row L to R: Alice Proctor, Phyllis Pointon,
Betty Egan, Mrs Goodwin.
Middle row L to R: Addie Dawson, Kitty Clowes,
Gladys Bailey.
Front row L to R: Alma Proctor, Mrs Turner,
Marjorie Twemlow.

W.I. fancy dress. *Back row L to R:* Mrs Turner, ?, Kitty Clowes, Dorothy Bourne, Alice Proctor, Addie Dawson, Merle Harvey, Gladys Bailey, Jennifer Bourne.
Front row L to R: Marjorie Twemlow, Phyllis Pointon, Alma Proctor with barrow.

The 60th Anniversary party of Brown Edge W.I. 1981 in the TAB.
Back row L to R: Gladys Lowe, Elsie Rowland, Nancy Harvey, Ethel Dawson, Elizabeth Lawton, Doreen Scott, Evelyn Forrester, May Poole, Eileen Sherratt, Annie Shallcross, Mrs Sirzuk, Lily Willis.
Front row L to R: Eva Turner, Mrs Bishop, Joan Berrisford, Hilda Simcock, Phyllis Pointon, Kitty Clowes.

W.I. fancy dress again.
Back row L to R: ?, ?, Pat Pickstock, Francis Biddulph, Gladys Lowe, Mrs Simmons.
Third row L to R: Alma Proctor, Harriet Hollins, Marjorie Twemlow, ?, Betty Egan, Addie Dawson, Alice Proctor.
Second Row L to R: Beattie Holdcroft, Lily Beckett, Gladys Bailey, ?, Ethel Dawson.
Front row L to R: Annie Mitchell, Kitty Clowes, Elsie Rowland.

W.I. visit to Spillers Flour.
Back L to R: Hilda Hollins, Gladys Bailey, Mrs Simmons, ?, Harriet Hollins, Mrs Simcock, Winnie Hodkinson.
Middle row L to R: Mrs Weaver, Alan Turner, Addie Dawson, Iris Turner, Mrs Pointon, Mrs Slack, Mrs Mountford, Dorothy Bourne, Maggie Hargreaves, Kitty Clowes, Mrs Turner, Mrs Hargreaves, Alice Cumberlidge, Annie Pointon, Anna Snape.
Front L to R: Annie Mitchell, Mrs Harvey, Mrs Powditch, Mrs Willott, Beattie Holdcroft, Mrs Mottram, Mrs Hodkinson, Mary Bowyer.

Tom Johnson

My father, Thomas Johnson Senior, was a soldier in the North Staffordshire Regiment, in the First World War. I have found out about his experiences. He himself never talked much about it. He used to say 'It's all in the past, forget about it.' He put his medals in a drawer and nobody ever saw him wearing them.

When I was young I used to get them out and polish them and look at them. My dad used to say 'Put 'em back in the drawer, they've never done me any good!'

He has been dead about forty years now and I just felt I wanted to know more about what had happened and how he came to get his five medals. They ended up in a trunk in the attic and were dirty, some with no ribbons on. Friends have helped me with the research and I am very grateful.

Dad won the Distinguished Conduct Medal for saving the life of an officer, Lieutenant Wint. The details of this were published in the London Gazette on March 28th 1918. The men had been on a raiding party. They used to go on daylight raids to German trenches, to capture prisoners, to take back to their own lines. The officers used to interrogate the prisoners, to find out what the enemy's plans were.

After one of these raids, Dad noticed this soldier lying down, badly wounded, in between the lines. The Sergeant said to Dad 'What are we going to do Corporal?' and Dad replied Oh, we'll go and fetch him'. When they were halfway there, the Sergeant was shot and had to turn back, because of his injuries. Dad went ahead on his own and reached a shell hole where, while being heavily bombed, he bandaged the wounded Lieutenant Wint. The German soldiers realised what he was trying to do and were shouting good luck to him.

Dad refused to surrender and realised they had to try and get back to their own lines. He was in charge of a Lewis gun which is bigger than a rifle, you had to set it on three legs. He realised that he could not carry the gun, and the wounded man. It was a big criminal offence to lose your gun but Dad put the soldier over his shoulder and left the gun behind. He managed to get back, despite enemy fire going off around him.

In the meantime they had brought up reinforcements and there was a new officer in charge who had had no experience. He said to Dad 'Where's your gun Johnson?' and the Sergeant said 'It's over there and we're not fetching it'. The officer put them both on a charge. They were court-martialled, Dad for leaving his gun and the Sergeant for disobeying the order of an officer. Of course they were let off and heard no more of it.

When they came to get their awards they had come straight from France, where they had been up to their knees in water, in the trenches. There were lots of them, officers and privates. It was pouring down with rain and they had to stand there, waiting for the King to come past. The King was going to present the medals and they had orders that when he came, they had to throw their hats up in the air three times and shout 'Hip, Hip, Hooray'. Dad said 'There's no fear I'm doing that', and the officer said 'You must do it or I'll put you on a charge'. They stood there about two hours, in the rain, then there came a message saying the King wasn't coming, he'd got a little cold. So another big army man came and took his place.

They had three weeks leave and a free pass for the train. Dad was in the same compartment as an officer from a Yorkshire regiment and they got into conversation and found they had been in some of the same battles. When they got to Stockton Brook Station there

The presentation of the clock to Corporal Thomas Johnson from the residents of Brown Edge, in appreciation of his gallant service in the First World War. *Standing:* Thomas Johnson, Joe Grindy, ?, ?, Harry Baggaley, Joe Gratton, ?. *Sitting:* Mrs Bentley, Mr Bentley, Major Dickinson, Mrs Dickinson.

Brown Edge soldiers World War 1 1914-18.
Back row L to R: E. Pickford, T. Goodwin, A. Hall, W. Willott, J.Hargreaves.
Middle row L to R: S. Simcock, W. Tomkinson, T. Jolley, S. Hargreaves.
Front row L to R: J. Simcock, J. Frost, Tom Johnson.

was a Brown Edge bobby standing there and he challenged Dad and the officer. He said 'Why aren't you over there fighting with the rest of 'em?' The officer was so angry he pulled his revolver out and threatened to shoot the policeman. He would have done it if it hadn't been for Dad. Dad just said 'Forget about it, it isn't worth it.' He left the officer and walked home to Brown Edge, through the fields, still covered in sludge from the trenches.

A couple of days later the policeman came to see Dad at home. He said 'I'm very sorry about the other day, I shouldn't have approached you like that. I thought that officer was going to shoot me!' Dad replied 'He would have done if it hadn't been for me. What you should have done was asked for my pass, it was in my pocket!' The policeman still felt that the officer should not have threatened him and said he was going to take it further. However nothing more was heard of the incident.

Dad said once when they were being shelled by the Germans the Army brought some young soldiers up. They all had dark hair but next morning, when the shelling had all died down, they found them dead and they had snow white hair. There were no signs of any wounds, it was just fright. When they turned them over, in the middle of their foreheads was a blue mark.

After the war someone got Dad a job driving, for Parker's Brewery, delivering beer to all the pubs. He married my mother, Ruth Beardmore, and they settled in Norton Green. His father's name was Jim Johnson and his mother was a Bourne before she got married.

Dad used to go to the Workingmen's Club in Brown Edge. He used to say 'In the old club there's been more wars fought and lost than ever there was in France and Belgium - and none of 'em had ever seen anything'.

Grandfather Johnson kept a shop, a mixed business, that used to be next to the Lump of Coal. We moved there when I was in my 20s, my mother and my sister, Enid, ran the shop. Opposite the shop, where Keith's supermarket is now, was a little toffee shop, Baddileys.

The Butchers shop which was situated next to the Lump of Coal, c.1905. It belonged to R Sheldon but later became Johnson's grocery shop. It was bought by the brewery and demolished in 1962.

A village procession at the end of World War I. It has
reached School Bank and the Headmaster's house
can be seen on the left.
Major Dickinson is in the centre of the picture.

Tom Johnson Senior in
First World War uniform.

The World War 1 medals awarded to Corporal Thomas Johnson:
The Distinguished Conduct Medal, 1914-15 Star, The British War
Medal, Victory Medal and Military Medal.

There was also a shop where Jack Crossley and his wife made their own pies, bread and cakes. Next to the Roebuck pub was Short Street, the only street on Brown Edge. There were three little cottages in the street, occupied by Mrs Morris, Percy Williams and Fred Turner. A chap named Jesse Dawson (Rozzer) lived where Syds' hairdressers is now, then Tom Mayer came after. A lot of families had nicknames because there were so many with the same surname. Our nickname was 'Mouse'.

Tom Johnson Senior and his wife, Ruth in front of Poolfield House. They were living in Heaton Villas at the time.

Mum and Dad had nine children but one died. Dad was living at 6, Heaton Villas when he died, aged 77 years. He had been presented with a clock from the people of Brown Edge, with 'For services to the Great War 1914-18' inscribed on it. Mother gave me the clock and the medals. They now have new ribbons on and have been mounted in a frame. As well as the Distinguished Conduct Medal (DCM), Dad had the World War One Trio which consists of the 1914-15 Star, the British War Medal and the Victory Medal. His fifth medal is the Military Medal. The DCM is the army's second highest military award. When Dad rescued Lieutenant Wint he had to leave his gun behind. Apparently if he had carried his gun he would have been awarded the Victoria Cross, but there was no way he could have carried both.

As there is so much interest in the wars now, my wife rang and told the Leek Post & Times about Dad's story. They came to see us and did a feature in the 'Advertiser'. We knew nothing about Lieutenant Wint, the officer Dad rescued. Dad never kept in touch with anyone after the war. It turned out that Jayne Wint, a great niece of Thomas Wint, lives in Leek. She read the article and went to the Leek Post & Times Office. Jayne had no idea that the son of the man who saved her great uncle was still alive, and living so near.

The Leek Post contacted me and arranged for us to meet, which we did. We exchanged tales and shared photos, a very emotional meeting. I now have a photo of my Dad, in uniform, his clock and the medals, mounted and framed, all up on the same wall. He was a very modest man and I feel very proud of what he did.

The meeting between Tom Johnson and Jayne Wint in 2005. It was arranged by the Leek Post and Times. Jayne is a great niece of Thomas Wint, the officer whose life was saved by Tom's father.

Gladys Bailey nee Bourne

I was born in 1919 at Lane Ends, in Top Heath Row. My parents were Ellen and William Bourne. Mother was an Allinson, before she was married, and came from Bagnall. Grandfather Allinson used to make coffins and Mother used to say she played amongst the coffins, when she was a girl.

My father was born on Brown Edge. He was a miner and walked to Whitfield and back every day. At Top Heath Row we lived with Grandad Bourne and Uncle Arthur Goodwin. There were nine of us: two boys and seven girls. There was Mary, Annie, George, Elsie, Hilda, Lizzie, Bill and Sarah. I was the youngest. We never did any fighting because Dad wouldn't have it.

My older sisters went to Leek, to work in the mills. They had to walk to Stockton Brook every morning for the train. There were no buses then, before Turners started. When it was dark Mother used to go over the Rocks with them. They carried jam jars, with candles in.

Heath Row and Top Heath Row were built by Robert Heath for his miners and they were well built houses.

I loved school. The headmistress at the infants was Mrs Garner and her assistant was Mrs Williams. I always liked reading. Mr Benton asked my mother if I could go to grammar school but she said no, she couldn't afford it. Mrs Heath used to run a little shop, near the school. It was beautiful and clean. I remember once I met Mr Benton and he asked me if I would like some sweets - he bought me a quarter from the shop. They were two pence and I thought I was the queen. He was a nice teacher and had a very good voice. We used to sing all the old country songs.

Walter Jones ran a woodwork class at night. Sometimes we had to sandpaper for the boys. He used to say 'Now look at it from all angles'. We also had to weed in the garden. There was only a pot stove at school but I never remember feeling cold. We always went home at dinnertime.

There always seemed a lot of children in the house but we were usually in bed when the older ones came in. Mother used to work on a farm at Trentham, before she was married. She liked nice things and kept everything nice. That's how you are when you've been in service.

When I left school I went to work in the mills. I went to work at Brough, Nicholson and Hall in Leek. I got eight shillings and four pence a week but my bus fare was ninepence a day. I had to catch Turner's bus at 7.15. I thoroughly enjoyed it, I never should have left. I was in the Samples Room but was only a runabout girl. There were two machinists, two cutters and an overlocker and they made samples to send to London, for fashion shows.

Later I went to work at Buller's in Norton Green Lane. I was fettling and a turner, just a factory girl. I didn't really enjoy it. I was ever so shy and got teased a lot. During the war I should have gone in the ATS or WRENS but the boss came in and said 'We've got you off because we make insulators for Russia!' They did not really want to lose their workers. Buses did go from Brown Edge, to take workers to Radway Green and Swynnerton, the ordinance factories.

I remember once Norton Lane was all snowed up, but no matter how bad the weather was, Turner's buses were always there. That's what we always relied on. In the morning the driver used to watch for me coming over The Rocks.

When I met my husband, Jack Bailey, he was an electrician in the mines at Norton. He lived in St Anne's Vale. He joined the RAF when he was 19 but before that he was in the Home Guard. An officer from Longsdon was over them. They did lookout duties at night, in a hut on Wood Bank, over Broad Lane way. They used to have a lot of fun. Jack used to tell me tales and laugh his socks off. I think there were five of them on duty. They had a stove in the hut and used to play cards. I think they'd have been frightened to death if they had seen anything.

A few of us used to walk, on a Sunday night to High Lane, where Haywood Hospital is. We just went to have a walk around and see the fellas. There was never any trouble, everybody just walked across there and back. It was called, the 'Monkey Run'. Our parents didn't know. They let us go to the Band Room but we had to come straight home. It was two hours of fun and laughter for sixpence.

We used to go to church three times on Sunday. It was morning service, Sunday School in the afternoon, then evening service. It was a way of life. I remember the Misses Heatons always sat in the same place in church. Major Dickinson was a big bug as well.

Once a year, in summer, the Sunday School used to go to Cumberlidge's fields by Hobbs House. We had an

Jack Bailey in R.A.F. uniform, c.1940.

apple or an orange, a present for being good. When it was the Chapel Charity we walked all round the village in the morning, and everybody went to Chapel at night. They used to have to get forms in for extra seating. The School Sports Day was another big day on the village. We all paraded round behind a banner. There was a prize for the best fancy dress. It was held in Durber's field, opposite Singlet Farm - a real village day, everybody was there.

When my husband Jack was about twenty he had a nasty accident. He was out shooting, with his dad, who belonged to a shooting club. They used to shoot ducks and rabbits. They were walking along, Jack was in front, some ducks flew up and they both put their guns up. Jack's father's gun went off before it should and shot Jack. Jack fell to the ground but recovered and got up again. His dad said if Jack hadn't got up he would have shot himself straight away. The pellets went through Jack's teeth and in his arms. He had pellets all over him. The Doctor said it would cause more trouble if he got them out. Jack always used to rub his skin, and it came up, and you could see all the pellets. Accidents will happen.

Since I married I have always lived in St Anne's Vale. I am still involved in Church and village activities. I was in the Mother's Union and have been a member of the Women's Institute for over fifty years. We've had some really good times, dressing up and doing plays and pantomimes. I've always enjoyed a good laugh and a bit of fun.

Mrs Martha Bailey nee Hargreaves with her three children.
L to R: Dorothy Rushton, Jack Bailey, Martha Bailey and Alma Proctor.

A trip in a charabanc for fireman officials from Norton Colliery.
Front row 6th from the left is John William Proctor and 5th is Albert Bailey.

Out for a day's shoot.
Left to right: 4th Mr Wilshaw, 5th Albert Bailey (Jack Bailey's Dad).

W.I. Desert Song.
Back row Sheiks L to R: ?, Nora Rolinson, Barbara Goodwin, Marion Woodward.
Middle row L to R: Gladys Bailey, ?, Lily Beckett, Betty Birkin, Doris Berrisford, Marjorie Twemlow.
Front row L to R: Mrs Brown, Mrs Bishop, Joyce Wedgewood, Marjorie Shone, Margaret Tatton.

Tree Planting in the Playing Fields.
Back row L to R: Harry Slack, John Barker, Ken Turner, Betty Barker, Jack Rushton, ?, ? .
Front L to R: Margaret Tatton, Elsie Alcock, Gladys Bailey, Colin Simcock, ?, Harry Hammond, Nancy Harvey, ?.
With spades: David Pass and Bill Bassnett.

Alma Proctor nee Bailey

I was born in 1918 at Rock House, St Anne's Vale. My father's name was Albert Bailey and my mother was Martha Hargreaves, before she was married. I had a brother Jack and a sister Dorothy. I was the middle one. I had a grandfather called John Bailey and my grandmother was Hannah Brandon. I never knew my grandmother Bailey.

My other grandparents were Charles and Ann Hargreaves. They had eight children: George, Martha, Charlotte, Florence, Charles, Enoch, Samuel and Nellie. They lived at Hodgfields before they came to Spout House, in Sandy Lane. I think my mother was born at Hodgfields. Grandfather always walked to work to the pit every day, there and back. My cousin, Kitty Clowes, still lives at Spout House.

My mother was the post woman before she was married. She used to go from Sandy Lane as far as Knypersley Mill and the Tower, every morning. She used to come home and dress-make - she used to make clothes for people on the village. When it was the Anniversary at Hill Top Chapel, she used to say she could count how many frocks she'd made for the children who were on stage.

We had a smallholding at Rock House. We always kept two pigs and would kill them and have fresh ones. We had one cow

Grandparents Charles and Ann Hargreaves at Spout House with their children Martha and Charles. Their other children were George, Charlotte, Florence, Enoch, Samuel and Nellie.

and also hens. I didn't help much; I didn't like animals that much. My mother's grandfather and great grandfather built the house and also the one attached, Avonglen. My mother's brother Enoch Hargreaves, used to live in this one.

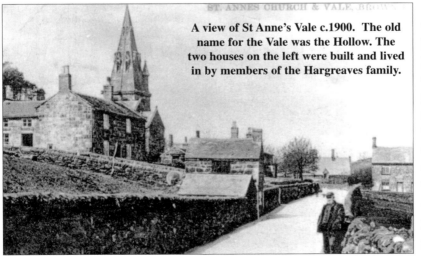

A view of St Anne's Vale c.1900. The old name for the Vale was the Hollow. The two houses on the left were built and lived in by members of the Hargreaves family.

I had diphtheria when I was three and had to go to Leek Hospital. Then, when I was six, I had scarlet fever and had to go to the Isolation Hospital in Tinster's Wood. There was an epidemic at the time and when Tinster's Wood was full they took the children to Leek. I had everything, except rheumatic fever, but my brother and sister had nothing. I remember they came to fetch me in a horse-drawn carriage. They burnt a block in the house to fumigate it and stoved all my belongings.

I was in there for six weeks and no-one could visit. I remember seeing my mother looking through the window. She was wearing a big hat. Before we came out we had to have a bath with carbolic soap. It was such a strong smell I can still smell it now. After the bath I could not go back in, so I had to stand outside, until my father came. We then walked home together down the long path from the wood.

I went to Brown Edge School, which was very near and I always liked school. I left at fourteen and got a job in a shop at Leek, in Derby Street. It was called J Bailey & Sons.

I went out at eight o'clock in a morning and got back at nine o'clock in the evening. I was doing alterations, because it was a draper's shop. I worked in the workroom and got six shillings a week, and did six days. My bus fare was four shillings and sixpence, so I had one and six pence left. They sold curtains and dress material, hosiery and underwear. Upstairs it was dresses and coats. The manager, Mr Percy Bailey, later asked me if I would go into the shop as well, for eight shillings a week. I used to go out and measure up for curtains and then come and make them up, in the workroom.

If they were busy in the shop they called me, and I had to run down two flights of stairs. I would serve a bit then run back up again. Once I was doing an order for Adams, and it wasn't done, so the manager told me off. My mother said I should give my notice in. Well I couldn't be upstairs making curtains and down in the shop as well, so I told him. He said, 'Oh no, in future if you're busy they must manage in the shop.' I stayed and worked my way up to two pounds five shillings a week. When Mr Bailey was away I was in charge and I had to lock up and do the cashing up. On Saturday night I had to take the money in a leather pouch to the night safe. There were crowds in Derby Street then, but I always felt safe; you wouldn't do it today.

When the war came we had to go to register at Broad Street, in Leek, for war work. I was excused because I was managing the shop, cashing up and everything. We were open until nine o'clock on Saturdays and I did not get home until ten o'clock.

I did not go out much because it was so late when I got home. There were dances at the Band Room but my parents would not have let me go anyway. My dad used to say, 'Girls bring their trouble home and lads take it somewhere else!'

I met my husband, Arthur Proctor, one Good Friday when there was a wakes at Knypersley Pool. He worked as a winder at Norton Colliery. He was conscripted into the army and went in April 1940. As he did not work on the coalface he was not exempt from war service. We were married at Brown Edge in January 1941, when he was on leave. He went back the following Friday and I did not see him again until November.

My dad was a fireman at Norton Colliery. One day he had an accident, had a blow to his chest. I remember he said, 'It would have killed plenty of men.' This was on the Sunday and he died the following Saturday, just sitting in his chair. He was 54

My family have lived in St Anne's Vale for generations. My brother, sister and myself were born here and have lived all our lives in The Vale. We were always a very close family.

Alma's husband, Arthur Proctor.
He was in the 1st Batallion
Herefords Regt. and took part in
the D Day landing 1944

Alma's mother Martha Bailey nee Hargreaves

The "Toothache Stone" at Knypersley Pool, c.1911. The young men
are *left to right:* Fred Proctor, Arthur Baggaley and Sam Bratt. This
stone is still there but has been moved to the bridge.

Sam Hargreaves – Martha's
brother c.1950.

A boxing bout. This photo was
taken in the wood that used to
be behind Spout House. The
enthusiasts used to come each
year to camp and practice.
Charles Hargreaves is on the
left and the person on the right
is Bill Matthews, Stanley
Matthew's father.

Y.M.C.A. Football Club pictured in St Anne's Vale 1951.
Back row L to R: W. Goldstraw, J. Rushton, A. Berrisford, S. Knight, D. Fox, E. Clowes, D. Berrisford, A. Willott.
Front row L to R: R. Knight, J. Johnson, A. Proctor, C. Dawson, C. Goldstraw.

The christening of Alma and Arthur's son John, 1949.
Standing L to R: John Proctor, Maud Rushton, Jack Bailey, Martha Bailey, Arthur Proctor, Jack Rushton, William Rushton,
Seated L to R:: Dorothy Rushton with Ann, Alma with John, Alice Proctor, Gladys Bailey with Susan.
Clive Proctor at the front.

Sammy Bratt
Audrey Buckley née Bratt

My father, Sam Bratt, was born in 1897. His parents were Sampson and Mary Ellen. Grandma's name was Bullock, before she was married, and she came from the True Blue pub at Milton. Her mother was a Goldstraw, from Wetley rocks.

Grandfather, Sampson Bratt, was about nine when his mother died, but he had a wonderful stepmother, called Sarah, and there were at least seven children to look after. In 1895 Grandfather opened a butcher's shop in Breach Road. It was next to his father Joseph's shop and post office. Then a couple of years later he had a house and shop built across the road, on the corner opposite the old Roebuck pub. Grandma and Grandad had four children, Mabel, Nellie, Samuel and Arthur.

Dad was in the First World War but he didn't talk much about it. We still have all the many postcards he sent from the Front. He wrote so much on them, and so neatly, and what a sense of humour he had. He adored his mother.

I think Dad met my mother when she used to play the organ in church. He used to work a pump to keep the organ going. Mother's name was Mountford, before she was married.

The four children of Sampson and Mary Ellen Bratt.
Left to right: Nellie, Mabel, Arthur and Sam.

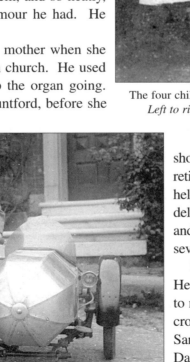

Sammy Bratt on his bike outside the Plough, Endon, 1920s.

Mother and Dad came to live at the shop in about 1928, when Grandfather retired. He went to live at Endon but still helped in the shop at weekends. I started delivering meat when I was about eight and was still delivering when I was seventy-six. This was when I retired.

Dad died in 1973 aged seventy-six. He loved his bike and motors. He used to race through the gates at Ford Green crossing - they used to say they were Sam Bratt's gates. They also said, when Dad started to rev up on his bike at Brown Edge, they used to step back at Norton Green. He was quite a character.

Joseph Bratt pictured at the Breach with one of his grandsons, on the horse.

Joseph Bratt seated in the garden.

The old Post Office in Sandy lane. This shop was built in 1846 by Sampson Bratt as a village store and bakery. The Post Office was added in the 1870s. Mr Joseph Bratt, postmaster, is standing in the doorway with his mother. The shop is now Helen Holdcroft's curtain and upholstery shop. It has changed very little.

Outside the Slaughterhouse at
Bratt's Butchers 1911.
Sam Bratt is on the left and Arthur, his brother,
is in the middle.

The house and shop of Bratt's Butchers.
It is now a private house. The land attached was
sold in 2004 and five three storey houses
built on the site.

Brenda Sargeant née Bratt

It was said of my father that 'All his prayer books had handles' meaning that pint pots were his prayer books, but he was a good, kind man. He was always ready to help anyone - even those who had wronged him.

Discussing religion, one Sunday morning, he said to me 'If you want to find a true Christian don't go to church, go to your nearest pub'. In time I realised the kindness and goodness to be found there.

Audrey and I weren't much age when we'd got our little white jackets on and our baskets, with the deliveries in. We hated going up to School Bank, they were all Pointons up there and I used to get the orders mixed up. We couldn't carry much at a time that's why we had to keep traipsing up there. When I was about thirteen, Audrey and I got a second-hand bicycle each, which was better for deliveries.

The family had two shops to run. The main one was at Smallthorne where Dad was at first. Grandpa Bratt used to look after the Brown Edge one then.

Sam Bratt outside the Smallthorne shop.

When Dad was a child he used to go to a dame school at Milton. This was where he pulled Susie Cooper's hair. He also went to Heaton's School at Brown Edge, and he did learn to play the violin. I think he was missing more often than not.

When he was a young man he used to take his pony and trap and pick up a gentleman at Rock Cottage, to take him to Endon Station. He used to hear the whistle at the top of Clay Lake, and then they went like the clappers. He never missed the train but it must have been hair-raising.

Mary Ellen Bratt, Sam's mother.

Grandma Bratt was a lovely lady. When it was the depression she'd trudge down Norton Green with a basket of meat. There were no fridges then and nothing was ever wasted. People used to say 'Mary Ellen we can't pay' and she'd say, 'You will when you can'.

A motorbike accident in 1926 had left Dad with a severely damaged leg, which he was unable to bend, leaving some people to think that it was wooden. He'd refused an operation, to straighten the leg, because it would have meant a long stay in hospital and who would mind THE SHOP - that always came first. Some of us used to call it 'That flaming SHOP!' but he would say, 'How will people manage without it?'

I later went to university and did not work in the shop. Once though I had to help out for six weeks, when mother was ill. She had had an operation. I was expected to know that one lady had her meat at cost, because she couldn't possibly have afforded to pay the proper price. I had got my price list and said the price, as it should be. She said it was a bit too much. Dad came over and said to me 'What are you doing, you johnny, you've got it all wrong!!' It wasn't my mistake but she would think it was.

Then there was a family that came in, last thing, for cracked eggs. We charged a halfpenny less. I'd been careful and we hadn't got any, so Dad sent me in the back to crack some. I spent ages trying to crack those eggs, I was fast running out of saucers. We had to use them up afterwards. 'All those wretched eggs,' I said to Dad. 'Why don't you let them have them for half a penny less instead of all this performance?' He said 'I couldn't do that because of their pride; their pride would be hurt."

Dad would rather have been an engineer though. He had that powerful motorbike that he rode about on and upset people, especially Grandad Mountford. There came a time when Dad had to go to Burslem, because there had been protests about the noise he made. He had to do a test drive through the town. He put a potato in the exhaust and rode quite quietly. He got away with it.

One day Mum told Dad that the best steak would have to go up to six shillings a pound and he said 'That's it - when I have to charge six shillings a pound for fillet steak, and people are buying my best lamb's liver for their poodles, it's time for me to retire!'

Dad is remembered for his exploits and his dares. A lot of his escapades we didn't hear about. He loved children though and was very kind to them. He would help anyone out, and that's how I remember him.

Sam Bratt with his daughter Brenda, c.1928.

Stephen Buckley

I was born in Woodland Avenue, Norton in 1953. My father was Gordon Buckley and my mother was Audrey Bratt. My father died suddenly, when I was six and Mother and I came to live in the house that I live in now, at the Breach. It was a cafe at one time, called Breach Café,

Mum went back to work in her dad's shop, Bratt's butchers, serving and delivering orders. I lived most of my life at the shop. Gran spoilt me and I grew up with tales of my grandfather, Sammy Bratt. Everybody had a tale to tell about Grandfather. His full name was Samuel Bullock Bratt - a good name for a butcher. He loved going to the markets, Newcastle on Mondays and Leek on Wednesdays. He rarely went on holiday - his holiday was going to the markets. He would do all his buying up, and then go up the town and have a drink, one too many probably. He would then get somebody to drive him back to Brown Edge. He wouldn't come home straight away though; he'd either go to the Hollybush or the Lump of Coal.

My grandma used to shout to me 'Stephen, where's your grandfather? Go and fetch him', so I'd look outside and see which pub the kids were standing outside; he'd be in that pub. As soon as he came out he'd throw a load of money up in the air, anything he'd got in his pockets. The children would pick it all up. It was a common event.

He was mad on motorbikes and had a passion for motors. He was mates with Sam Turner and wanted to go into transport with him. He wanted his father to lend him some money, but his father said 'No way am I going to lend money for something which is going to take people off the Village'. He was thinking of his own business.

Grandad loved a bit of fun and was always up for a dare. There was a bloke who kept some pigs and someone dared Grandad to go in the pigsty and paint the pigs black. Course he did, and next day the bloke came running across to Grandad's, 'You'll have to kill these pigs, something's wrong, they've gone black overnight.' The things Grandad used to do for bets! He swam across Rudyard Lake one night, for a bet. It nearly killed him. He was halfway across and they had to get a boat out to fetch him back. He said if it hadn't been for the beer he'd have been a goner, it kept him afloat and kept him warm.

He was mad on boxing, he loved it. At Belle Vue one night the bloke was knocked out in the first round. They all bet Grandad to get up in the ring; they had a collection. The boxer knocked him all round the ring, but he did it. He went through the Roebuck on a horse one day. They dared him and he went in one door and out of the other. There was no harm in Grandad. He'd help anybody but I wouldn't like to have crossed him. He always wanted to go into transport but he ended up going into his father's butcher's shop. He never really wanted it.

Bratt's also had a butcher's shop in Smallthorne. If the shop ran out of meat, they used to send some on Turner's bus. It was in a basket and they used to get them to stop outside the shop and drop it off. Grandad always looked after people who were Brown Edgers and regulars in the shop. People did stick together, as hard as times were. Things were very tight when meat was on ration. One night Grandad was going to the dog track. He was keen on greyhounds and used to rear them. He was meeting someone, a bit cloak and dagger like. He'd got him some meat from Manchester way. Grandad parked the motor up, went into the dog track, met the bloke, and loaded the meat up. They then went to watch the races.

When Grandad came out, there was a policeman standing by his van. He thought that was it. If you got caught it was a serious thing and you went to prison. The policeman said, 'Is this your van sir?' Grandad said, 'Yes'. The policeman then said 'Well, you've got a flat tyre. I'll help you to change it, I can see you're on your own'. Grandad had got all this meat covered up in the back and the policeman was helping him. 'Thank you very much,' Grandad said and headed home. He used to hide the meat everywhere in the shop, even in the corn bins.

Grandad was a brilliant businessman but Gran did all the bookings and sorting the money out. Every time Grandad went to a sale Gran was terrified about what he would buy next. He bought farms and property all over the place. He even bought a street of houses once, in Hanley. Property was very cheap then.

There was another story about a bloke who was desperate to get in the army but didn't know his left from his right. Grandad said, 'Right we'll fix this'. They got a battin of straw and a battin of hay and tied straw to one leg and hay to the other. They had the bloke marching up and down saying 'straw, hay… left, right'. It was just harmless fun.

A chap called Burgess who kept the Hollybush had a little lad who was very small. Grandad said to him 'We'll have you right. We've got just the thing for you, you want some muck in your shoes. We'll make you grow. Muck makes anything grow, you ask any gardener, muck makes you grow.' They filled his shoes full of muck put his feet in and he went down home. Next time my grandad went down the Hollybush the lad's mother belted him round the head with a beer tray and nearly knocked him out.

After Grandad died I was thrown in at the deep end and started in the shop. It was always hard work and long hours, but we enjoyed it. Grandad died when I was about nineteen. When I got married, my wife Janet got on like a house on fire with Gran. Gran still did all the cooking and booking. She died at the age of eighty-nine, still at the shop.

We were busy in the shop but it was a major event Saturday, with a lot of people coming in and having a chat. An old chap called Harvey Durber used to pop in regularly to give Gran stuff to make jam with. The first thing he'd say was 'Hast any news? Who's died?' Two or three times he told us somebody had died and they hadn't. He was most put out when he found they hadn't died. He'd say 'I'd heard he'd died'. I remember one day he said, 'All as I'd like know is if I could find out the day I'm going to die'. When we asked him what he wanted to know for, he said 'Well I wouldn't get up that day, I'd stop in bed'. He was certainly our most colourful character. He went into Rock Cottage Nursing Home and died a few years ago.

Janet and I finished in December 2003. Neither of our sons were interested in taking over so it was sold and is now a private house. It had been Bratt's Butcher's shop for over a hundred years.

Stephen and Janet Buckley on their retirement outside the shop, 2003. The headline in the Sentinel was 'Bratt's gets chop after 100 years of business'.

Brenda Bratt as the Carnival Queen,
1935. The pageboys are Derek
Berrisford and Billy Schofield.

Harriet Bratt, wife of Sam,
with her two daughters.
Brenda is on the left and Audrey
on the right, c.1945.

A First World War army camp.
Sam Bratt is seated first on the right. He was a
trooper with the 4th Reserve Regiment of
Dragoons. They were based at Beaumont
Barracks, Queens Bay..

Arthur Bratt on the left and Sam, his brother,
seated. They both served in the First World
War. The date on the picture is 1st July 1917.

Brenda married Desmond Errol Sargeant in 1955 at Brown Edge Church. Her father, Sam is 3rd on the right and her mother, Harriet is first on the right. Mr and Mrs Harry Sargeant are on the left. The bridesmaids are Christine Midwinter, left and Barbara Bratt on the right.

Audrey nee Bratt and Gordon Buckley on their wedding day at Brown Edge church.

A holiday, with Turner's Bus Company. Alan Turner is at the back.

Another outing from the village probably to Wedgwoods and in the 1960s.

Noreen McIntyre nee Turner

I was born at the top of Fiddlers Bank, in 1925. My father was Reg Turner and my mother was Ada Rhodes, before she was married. She came from Alsagers Bank. Dad had an accident in the pit, and he bought Sparrowbill Cottage with his compensation. I have lived here all my life, apart from about eight years. Dad was born up the little lane by Apple Tree Farm. He had two sisters, Mabel and Doris.

Dad was Secretary of Brown Edge Working Men's Club for ten years. He liked it but he only got about £2 summat a week. This was the old club in Sandy Lane. Mother went every night and brought the money home. Dad used to put the barrels on tap, at dinnertime. If there was no steward, the Secretary had to do these jobs. There was a man who lived where Syd's hairdresser's is and I think his name was Jesse Dawson. He used to come and look after the stove pot in the Club. The men were always playing cards and billiards. They also had agricultural shows in there.

A new club was built, where Poolfield House was. It used to get packed at one time, when Mr Slater was there. If you weren't there for seven o'clock you couldn't get a seat. There was a big concert room with a billiards table. The clubs gone now and houses are there.

Noreen's mother, Ada Turner nee Rhodes.

When I was about eight I had scarlet fever and had to go to the fever hospital at Leek. I remember doing a lot of cork wool. I did yards of it. We used to sew it together to make slippers. I was in there for six weeks.

I went to Endon Secondary School in 1939 when it first opened. It was the best time of my life. I loved it. I only went from Easter to Christmas, then I had to get a job because I was fourteen.

I applied for a job with Swettenhams. They had a shop up Smallthorne and I thought I'd love to work there. I'd done a bit of an exam, but I had to wait til they'd got a vacancy. Mother said, 'I'm fed up of you being at home - you can go back to school'. So she sends me back, with a letter. The headmaster, Mr Ingley, said 'Everybody wants to leave school and your mother sends you back. How would you like to go in the canteen?' I said, 'Yes I don't mind.' It was an experiment run by the cookery teacher, Miss Bentley, to start doing school dinners.

There was just one woman, Mrs Lomas, who was the cook,

Noreen aged eleven.

John Wilshaw, Noreen's great-uncle, pictured on
Fiddlers Bank.

Noreen aged seventeen.

Five gentleman smokers.
Standing left to right: Lew Pointon and George Turner.
Sitting left to right: Noreen's dad Reg Turner, Fred Sheldon and Levi Fox.

Group of boys who look as if they are going on an outing, with their labels on. Middle row: 3rd from left, Roy Tyler. 4th from left Len Turner, Noreen's brother.

RIGHT: A Pile of pennies at the Roebuck.
L to R: Carrie Bourne, Harold Bourne, Mabel Dean, ?, Annie Berrisford, Jack Rushton, Diane Lawton, Horace Hayes, Lottie Hayes.

BELOW
Holiday outing to Clacton.

Back row L to R: 1st Fred Durber, 3rd Harry Hammond, 7th Bill Scragg, 9th Bill Simcock, 11th Sam Ellis, 13th Reg Turner, 16th Mr Bassnett.

Front row L to R: 1st Mary Durber, 5th Ethel Bird, 6th Gladys Hammond, 9th Winnie Ryles, 12th Annie Scragg.

and they used to send in two girls to help her. We had to clean a great big tub of potatoes. I used to make forty pints of custard a day, in two great big iron saucepans. I made two or three loads of pastry - six pounds at a time, by hand. There were no machines.

During the war, when the evacuees came, we were catering for three hundred and fifty a day - just the two of us. We had some help off the children. I got ten shillings a week. We had a big double gas cooker. We did meat and potato pie. Bratt's used to bring the meat and we did the pies in big oval dishes - ten portions in each.

One day Mrs Lomas fell, coming to work. Mr Ingley came and said, 'I'll send two girls in to help you. You'll have to do dinner on your own today!' Oh God, I'd never been so scared in my life, my knees were knocking together. Mr Ingley said, 'We'll have something easy - we'll have salmon pie and potatoes'.

I worked hard there. It didn't take me long to clean up and do all the dishes. The boiler we did the potatoes in - we used it to boil the teacloths in every night. I can only remember doing cabbage for vegetables. When the evacuees came, the boiler we used for the potatoes was full of lobby then. It makes me laugh now when I'm thinking about it. They were grand dinners for a shilling a day. The lads used to come, in the afternoon, asking for leftovers.

I left the canteen when I was seventeen. I was getting seventeen shillings and sixpence then and girls in the mills were getting thirty shillings. I went to Wardle and Davenports at Leek. I was joining seams on fully-fashioned stockings. I went a bit dizzy one day and sat down, on an orange box, with my head in my hands. The boss came through the door and gave me a minute's notice. He didn't listen to any explanation.

I went straight up and got a job at Brough's and it was a smashing job. We made school caps for Leek High school. Then I got promoted to making sports caps for England, out of velvet and cord.

Dad finished at the Club and went to keep the Foaming Quart pub. I was about seventeen then. Wilshaw's were there before us. There were four bedrooms and it was a cold, damp hole then. There wasn't a proper bar. As you went in, at the front door, the stairs used to go up. We had to wash the glasses up in a bowl. We had no water on at all, but there was a well across the road, right opposite. We had them many tubs, in the back kitchen, full of water.

Mum was the mainstay of the place; they called her Ada, everybody did. The floors were red and blue bricks and we had to do them on our hands and knees. They would never dry up. The kitchen had got great big hooks where we used to hang the pigs. The barrel was on a wooden stillage and we had to tap it. Dad showed me how to do that. I could do it and never spill a spot.

We made about a penny on a pint of beer. We used to get packed at the weekends. Dad had a stage built and put a piano on. The man who played the piano was called Benny and he came on Saturday and Sunday nights. We closed at ten o'clock but in summer there was an extension to ten-thirty. Sometimes the Bobbies used to be in, checking the closing time, and people used to scarper.

There were wooden forms all round. The pot stoves always smoked - we used to have to have the doors open. It was hard work for my mother. My brother, Len, had a thousand hens at one time, and we had pigs and calves. There was always a big saucepan on the fire, boiling potatoes peelings, for feed.

The wedding of Hilda Turner at Brown Edge Church.

I was twenty when I married Jack McIntyre. He came from Ball Green. Dad didn't want me to get married. It was a busy pub and I helped behind the bar. It was 1945 and rations were on. There was on old man, at the farm opposite, called Hargreaves. His daughter Ann did all my catering for me. I borrowed a wedding dress off my friend, Mary Bowyer. It was pale pink, it was lovely. I had Vera Moses' veil. We never had any photos taken - we couldn't afford. We had Harry Hammond's taxis and the reception at the pub. Jack and I both had to wait on. Dad gave a firkin of beer away. They heard down the road we were giving beer away and it was packed.

One day, Mr Boniface, from Parker's Brewery, came and asked us if we wanted to go and keep the Rose and Crown, at Hill Top. We left the Foaming Quart and it closed, as a pub. It later became Varsovia Lodge. We took over from Berrisford's at the Rose and Crown.

I remember when we were there Dad used to let 'The Marauders' group practice there, one night a week, when they first started. I'd never heard such a din in me life. Brayford's came after us and later Harry Frost.

Mum and Dad went back living up Fiddlers when they left the Rose and crown. Dad died when he was sixty-nine and mum went in a bungalow down Sytch Road. She was eight-six when she died.

Noreen's grandmother Elizabeth Turner.

The Hollins' children outside Hollins' shop, at Lane Ends (Church Road). This shop later became known as Joe's shop, after Joe Cumberlidge, who married Alice Hollins. It was demolished in about 1982. Bill and Alice are standing and Norman is seated.
The children's mother Esther and Noreen's grandad Turner were brother and sister.

Joy Adams nee Berrisford

I was born at the Rose and Crown pub, Hill Top, in 1932. My parents were Fanny and John Berrisford. Dad's mother, Sarah, used to keep the pub before us. Before that she kept a grocer's shop in Sandy Lane. She left there because when times were hard so many folk owed her money, with having stuff on tick - that's how the story goes. They had a bake house there and made bread.

Dad's mother's name was Frost, before she was married, and her father, John Frost, kept the Blue Pig at Ridgeway. Mum and Dad were married at Rushton Chapel and had six children: May, Fanny (died when she two) Jack, Fred, Ivy and eleven years after, Joy. Dad was fifty-eight when I was born.

I think Dad was born at 'The Moss', somewhere down Edge Lane. He was a joiner and worked for firms in the Potteries. The family are said to have come from South Staffordshire originally. They came to work in the mines here. There were always a lot of people on the village with the same surname and so they were given nicknames. No one seems to know who first started it. Our family's nickname was 'Muck' then there were 'Pups' and 'Bladers'.

John Frost who kept The Blue Pig, at Ridgway, in about 1860. His daughter Sarah was mother to John Berrisford, Joy's Dad.

Mother was stricter than Dad. Dad used to love going round the fields, mushrooming, shooting and fishing. He had a big garden. Where the car park is now, at the Rose and Crown, he had five or six greenhouses. He grew tomatoes, stick beans and flowers. People from the village used to come to buy tomatoes. Slacks in Burslem used to have lilies from him. I'm no gardener, but my brother Jack took after him.

John Berrisford in one of his five greenhouses at the Rose & Crown

Sarah Berrisford, nee Frost, Joy's Grandmother.

Dad used to love carving walking sticks. He used to go in the woods for his sticks. I think holly was a good one. He used to copy pictures out of books and sit hours chipping away with a penknife. He sold a lot of them to people who came from the Brewery, and one to

Lord Dewar. I still have some of his sticks now. He carved a scene all down the stick; dogs chasing rabbits, fashion in ladies dresses and examples of pottery ware, were just a few. He painted them as well.

I remember it was always very smoky in the pub. We all had to help serving the ale, mopping up and washing glasses. It was only beer; there was no spirits licence then. There was a little table at the back of the bar with two jugs on. One was for bitter and one was for mild. We used to draw the beer straight out of the barrel into the jugs. The beer came from Parker's Brewery, in Burslem and sometimes we used to run out. We had to close then.

We used to take the beer, in the jugs, through to the taproom. There was always a card table going and skittles. They were mad on cards and skittles. Towards the end of our time, there were a few ladies, but it was usually all men. They were mainly locals but there was a bus on

Meda and Edna Pointon c.1917. Meda, on the right, married Tom Adams in 1930 and was the mother of Ian Adams, Joy's husband.

Joy's dad, John Berrisford, as a young man. He was born in 1874 and died in 1952. He kept The Rose and Crown pub with his wife Fanny.

John Berrisford with his two sons: Fred in the centre and Jack (Jacker) on the right. Fred was killed in 1942 in Tobruk, in North Africa.

Saturday, from Burslem, and Burslem folk used to come up then. They seemed to quite like it.

We opened at ten o'clock in the morning and shut at two o'clock. Then we opened six until ten at night. There was a little bar but it was in the passage way; a few people sat in there sometimes. There was one main room. There was a little parlour but it wasn't used much.

There was a scorebook under the bar for those who couldn't pay. We scored fags up as well as beer. They settled up weekly, more often than not, when they had their wages.

I remember we had to fetch water from Star Well before water was piped. I remember Mrs Higgins sweet shop within Harvey's Mission.

When I went to St Anne's School Mr Jennings was the headmaster of the juniors. I went to Westwood Girls High School when I was eleven, and I never thought then that I would end up teaching at St Anne's. I went to Watford College then taught at Birches Head. I taught at Brown Edge for thirty years, from 1962 to 1992. I still help now, doing voluntary work.

From when I had been to school there, to when I went teaching at St Anne's, the school had hardly changed. Mr Fisher was head of juniors and Lilla Peak (Mrs Brereton when married) was head of infants. I taught the first class of the Infants, Mrs Clowes did the middle class and Christine Bailey taught the top class. Mrs Brereton used to teach as well. There was no secretary then and the Head had to do all the money and office work.

The schools were amalgamated in 1982 and Mr Ellis got the headship for two years. Then John Pye came and I liked him because he was strict and kept them in order. I think when they joined all the classes the Infants lost its identity. They expect too much of the infants when they are with the older ones. They had more pastoral care when it was just infants. We always used to see that they had their coats on and were properly wrapped up before they went out. Now they just go rushing out.

I think the classes were much better behaved. How they argue back now: if they don't feel like doing something they say so. Well you wouldn't dare to do that in the past. I think now they don't want to listen sometimes because the subjects are too advanced for the young ones. When I taught there we used to do basics in the morning, maths and English. In the afternoon we had a story, did nursery rhymes, singing, playing a record or cutting out, a lot of the fun things. Now its science, history and geography. There are no blackboards now, just electronic whiteboards. The children used to love sitting round the board and putting an answer on themselves, with a piece of chalk. They have a computer suite now. All changes are not for the best, I don't think.

I married Ian Adams in 1954. He used to live at Lions Paw Farm. His father, John

Joy and Ian Adams on their wedding day in 1954, in front of the Rose and Crown, showing the original entrance and the Parker's Ales sign.

Valley Head Infants Staff in 1973. *L to R standing*: Dorothy Rushton, Annie Mitchell, Rosemary Dickinson, Betty Hall, Carol Beech, Doris Bowden, Addie Dawson.
Seated: Cynthia Clowes, Joy Adams, Lilla Brereton, Christine Bailey, Joyce Brereton.

Adams, was a bus driver for Turners. His mother's name, before she was married, was Meda Pointon. Her parents kept the shop, in High Lane, before Garners had it.

My brother Fred was killed in the war, in 1942. He was in Tobruk, in North Africa. Brother Jack, or 'Jacker' as everyone called him, was a countryman through and through. He went to work, when he was fourteen, for John Holdcroft at Judgefields Farm and lived in there. He used to do hedge laying and went in for competitions for it. Old John Holdcroft was a very interesting man and a real craftsman. What he did was right and he instilled that in our Jack. Jack always used to quote him and say, 'Old John used to say…'. Jack married Hilda Heath and they bought the Colliers Arms at Hill Top, when it ceased to be a pub. There was a little field with it and a pool in the corner, which he made into a big garden. Jack had greenhouses, like my dad, and grew loads of tomatoes and runner beans. He spent all his time in the garden and had great big hedges all around to cut. He loved his garden, it was his life. He died in 2003 and Hilda, his wife, in 2005.

The house where Jacker Berrisford lived with his wife Hilda. It used to be The Colliers Arms, and closed in 1954.

The Pointon family outside their shop in High Lane, 1928, this shop later became Garners.
L to R: Lewis, Harry, Sarah, Meda and Edna. The mother Sarah's maiden name, was Scarlett.

BELOW LEFT
May on the left and Ivy, Joy's sisters. This is taken in the garden of the Rose and Crown. The cottage behind is where "Jacker" was born. It was later demolished.

BELOW RIGHT
Joy aged five with her guinea pigs.

St Anne's Panto, Sleeping Beauty 1965.
Front row L to R: Ann Adams, Julie Brereton, Susan Rolinson, Katherine Selby, Julie Litherland, Diane Cooper.
2nd row left to right: Gary Hargreaves, Steven Hughes, Paul Whiston, Susan Adderley.
3rd row L to R: John Gorman, Carol Berrisford, Andrew Poole, Peter Gregory, Janet Scott, Jill Snape, Simon Lewis.
Children with puppets: Martin Stone, David Adams, Chris Evans, David Pass, Pam Bartlem, ?.

St Anne's School Staff c.1989.
Back row L to R: Betty Hall, Joy Adams, Carol Burton, Carol Beech.
Sitting L to R: Cynthia Clowes, Viv Laws, Phil Craddock, Christine Bailey, Audrey Holdcroft.

St Anne's football team 1968/69. *Back row L to R:* Paul Rigby, Gary Hargreaves, Peter Gregory, David Painter, Graham Slack, Ian James, Graham Chadwick, David Adams, Mr Owen.
Front L to R: Christopher Lear, Ian Willott, Malcolm Dawson, Peter Whiston, Michael Matthews, Keith Johnson, Keith Nixon.

Table tennis in the TAB c.1946. Jack Bailey ready to play. Ian Adams, Joy's husband, 2nd from right.

Nora Rolinson née Sherratt

I was born in 1930, in a cottage up Fiddlers Bank. My Great, Great Grandfather Turner built the house; well, all the family helped. They also dug a well and we supplied a few houses around. It was beautiful water.

When I was married I went to live in the village, at Bank End. You couldn't see nothing down there to what you can see here. I missed it. Although Dad used to say 'Never try and grow anything higher than four inches up here. The wind will blow it down.'

My father's name was Albert Herbert Sherratt but they called him Herbie. He was known all over the village. He was born in St Anne's Vale. His father's name was Hugh. My mother, before she was married, was Rachel Turner and her parents were George and Mary Ann.

My family were always involved in the brass bands. There were two bands at one time. One was run by the Turners and Grandad Turner was in that. The Sherratts were in another one. I was always brought up with music. I was about five when I walked in front of the band, as their mascot. I had to wear a little outfit: I've still got the cape.

The band used to practice in the old Roebuck pub, as it was. They had a room upstairs. Later they practised in the Band Room, a wooden hut, down High Lane. We used to go to all the local carnivals and the memorial services, and do the charity Sundays. Then there was the Hospital Saturday, with the carnival and well-dressing. That was brilliant. On Christmas and Boxing Day mornings the band used to go all round the village, playing carols.

There were no women in the band. I never got to play anything. My uncle was teaching me to play piano but I was more interested in the lads outside. Uncle said it was either the lads outside or piano, so I went for the lads outside.

When it was the coronation, in 1937, the band was booked to play at Wetley Rocks, but we just managed to get back in time to play at Brown Edge as well. Turner's bus dropped us

St Anne's School all dressed up for the Coronation of King George VI and Queen Elizabeth, May 1937.

on School Bank and we got to Marshes Hill in time to play 'God Save The King' before Granny Knight lit the Bonfire.

I remember when I was about five I used to go to the Band Room with my mum and dad and sister May. My mother used to be on the refreshments counter. We used to do tea, sandwiches, cakes and things like that.

My dad used to be in the band, which was on a little stage. Uncle Arthur and sister May were on the piano accordion, Rene was on the piano and a friend from Baddeley Green was on the violin. They always played for the dances there. I was just pottering about, in the way part of the time.

There was a pot stove at both ends. When the men came in, after they'd had a drink up the road, they used to all stand round the stove, to have a warm. It used to be packed out. I think it was about sixpence at first, to go in. There was a bench at one end with refreshments on, and the stage was at the other end.

When we came out of the Band Room at night me and my sister used to carry my dad's big drum up from Sandy Lane to the top of Fiddlers. Imagine that in the winter time, carrying that up there. Dad used to give us sixpence for doing that.

People used to come from all the villages around, to the Band Room, on a Saturday night. There was a little bit of trouble sometimes. I won't give any names of them that caused it. It wasn't trouble like there is today.

Arkinstall's kept a music shop up Duke Bank and they took over on a Saturday night, when we finished. Mr Arkinstall used to play records.

May with her piano accordion, 1944. She always played this on Saturday nights at the Band Room.

Dad was in the First World War but he didn't talk about it much. He won the Military Medal. In the Second World War he was in the Home Guard. When he was on duty we used to go across at night to the hut at Wood Bank, to take Dad his supper. When evacuees came to the village we weren't going to have one, because we hadn't got the room, to be honest. All of a sudden my dad turned up with this little girl. He said nobody seemed to want her, so he brought her home, and she was with us for four years. Her name was Edith Ditchfield and she came from Manchester. The families of the evacuees used to come, on a coach, about once a month, to see them.

Edith was about ten and she went straight to Endon School, with our May. May was one of the first to go to Endon School. I was still at Brown Edge School, but there were a lot of evacuees there. We only did half days at school then, mornings one week then afternoons the next. This was to make room for these evacuees. Sometimes the teachers took us for walks down Tongue Lane or over to Biddulph Moor,

We got on a treat with Edith and her family when they came. We kept in touch afterwards. I remember once there was an air raid. Planes were going over to bomb Manchester and the sky was all lit up with incendiaries. This particular night Dad was up the garden with some binoculars. All of a sudden there was this big bang and me and my sister ducked under the table. Dad came running down saying 'Don't worry, it's alright, somebody's dropped something up Biddulph Moor'. It turned out to be a land mine.

We used to go to Hill Top Chapel every Sunday, and afterwards we decided to go a walk up to Biddulph Moor, to see where this mine had dropped. We were in our Sunday best. We only had new clothes for the Anniversary. It was a great big crater and we got in to find some bits. We got some, thought they were fantastic, came back home and got a good smack. The clothes were absolutely filthy with mud; that was the end of that.

Once an American plane crashed, over Wood Bank, near Henridding Farm. I was working and when we got home the first thing we did was to go and have a look. It was a right wreck. My sister and a friend had been coming up New Lane and it passed right over them, bits dropping off it. They went straight across to see it and it was a real blaze. The Home Guard were fetched out, to make sure no-one pinched any bits off it. No-one was injured. There were four men and a woman in it, but they got out and over the bank. Sam Bratt was up there pretty quick and climbed on the wing. He said he had to see if there were any poor blokes inside, but they were already safe.

Dad was a miner at Whitfield and he worked shifts. Lightning struck the house once. It was on a Friday and Dad was in bed. It did quite a bit of damage. It fetched the electric meters off in one room and sent them straight through the door, into the fireplace in the other room. I was at work at the time. I worked at Leek and I didn't know till I got home. There were no phones in those days. On the Monday, Dad went to see the insurance bloke. It was coming back in this bloke's car that he had a massive stroke and died. He was fifty-four. Doctors always said it was the shock from the lightning that had done it.

I remember, when we were little, every Sunday, after Chapel, May and I used to visit our great grandparents who lived at the bottom of Hough Hill. This was Great Grandfather Ephraim Sherratt and Great Grandmother Caroline. She always did a saucepan of soup for us and Great Grandfather had a silver case with sweets in. There was a choice of liquorice or mint but we could only have one each.

I left Endon School at fourteen and went to work at Wardle and Davenports at top of Mill Street in Leek. I worked on nylon stockings, putting them in pairs, then they went to be boxed up. It was 1944 and I remember we had a couple of air raids and we had to go down to the shelters in Leek. I stayed there until I was taken ill in 1950. I had tuberculosis and went into City General Hospital for thirteen months. I went to the mill again afterwards until 1960 when my daughter, Susan, was born.

When I was courting with Fred, we used to be in a gang, about twelve of us. We all used to go dancing or to the cinema in Hanley. There were tea dances at the old Lewis arcade and the Regent. Sometimes we went to the Coliseum in Burslem. Sometimes it was Belle Vue,

The two sisters with their evacuee friend, Edith Ditchfield, in the centre 1940. Nora is on the right and May is on the left.

Sherratt family group, Father and three children, 1945. *Standing:* Emma and Arthur *Seated:* Father Hugh and Albert Herbert. Emma married George Davenport and lived in the Vale all her life.

speedway in the afternoon and dancing at night. We were never late back and we used to go to the little café in Breach Road. We used to sit round the fire in the café and have tea and a piece of cheese on toast. It was great in the winter time. We used to have lots of fun.

My sister and I both returned to Fiddlers Bank. We live next door to each other, in the family home. We weren't away long. We love the sense of freedom and the amazing views.

Nora's Dad in front of the Foaming Quart, c.1945.
The pub closed in 1956 and became a private residence. A family called Zameriski lived there and it was renamed Varsovia Lodge. It later re-opened as a pub restaurant in 1978. This business closed in 2005.

Grandma Mary Ann Turner and Grandad George Turner c.1930.

The Sherratt Family. *L to R:* Nora's Grandma Hannah, baby Arthur (Nora's brother), Albert Herbert (Nora's dad), and Great Grandma Caroline.

BELOW:
A group of dancers in the grounds of Rock cottage c.1908. Nora's mother, Rachel Turner, is 4th from the left in the middle row.

The band playing at Wetley Rocks for the Coronation 1937.

Club Day – the band in Leek Market Place, c1937.
Nora in front with Uncle Arthur on the right. Dad is behind Arthur.

Well Dressing Sandy Lane, 1937. Nora's dad, Herbie is in the centre of the picture giving a speech.
Spout House can be seen in the background.

May's 21st birthday in the Band Room, 1947.
Seated L to R: Jean Mayer, Eileen Pointon, Arthur Sherratt, Nora, Frank Poole,
May, Herbert (Dad), Rachel (Mum), Auntie Emmie.

Leek and District Home Guard c.1941. Nora's dad is 6th from the left on the back row.

A good time at Blackpool in c.1950.
Back row L to R: Jack Rudge, Alan Turner, ?, Les Roberts, Fred Rolinson, Harry Simcock, Ken Bassnett, Bill Dale, Harry Turner, Frank Poole, Nora Rolinson, Marie Redfern, Ivan Redfern, ?, Eric Fox, Ray Simcock.
Middle row L to R: Keith Berrisford, Eric Holdcroft, Nancy Simcock, Arthur Simcock, Derek Berrisford, Francis Berrisford, Margaret Adams, Doreen Simcock, George and Ann Zameriski, ?, Violet Simcock.
Front L to R: May Poole, Hilda Simcock, ?, Roy Turner, Marjorie Roberts, Rachel Sherratt.

W.I. members at their Group meeting – Red Shadow. *L to R:* ?, Marian Woodward, Nora Rolinson, Mrs Bishop, ?, Betty Birkin, Barbara Goodwin, Marjorie Shone, Lily Beckett, Joyce Wedgwood.

Hill Top Chapel Concert Party - the Pied Piper. Both pictures
Left to right: Philip Buxton, Roy Cottrell, Clive Simcock, Glyn Buxton, Julie Cottrell and on his knees at the front, Mick Buxton. This group entertained for a number of years and performed at different local venues.

Left to right: Susan Rolinson, Elizabeth Painter, Reg Halfpenny, Ann Buxton, Peter Bowyer

Betty Walklett née Goodwin

I was born in 1911 at Hill Top, just past Broad Lane. My father was Mark Goodwin and my mother was Alice Gibson, before she was married. I would have liked to have been called Alice. I was actually christened Eliza, after my Auntie, but I hated it. I couldn't tell you how much I hated that name, so I called myself Betty and it's stuck with me.

Grandad Gibson kept a little shop at Hill Top, just above where Dad lived. It was also a smallholding, I remember them haymaking. They also kept horses and hens. Mrs Davenport lived in the cottage above. I had an older brother called Mark and one called John. There was also Nathan, who was a bit backward. He was probably called after Grandad Gibson.

Mother was ill for three years and then died, at the age of forty-five, and the family was split up. I was sent to my Granny and Grandad Gibson, who kept the shop. John went to Grandad Frost and Mark stayed at home with Nathan and my dad. Mark and Dad both worked at Chatterley Whitfield.

My Granny and Grandad Gibson gave me all the love in the world. I had none off Dad. Granny used to go to Burslem, in a horse and float, and buy papers, tinned stuff, lots of different bottles of sweets, and all odds and ends for the shop. I used to pinch some of the sweets. When a big collier's strike came, Granny let a lot of stuff out on tick, and eventually she was bankrupted because of that. I remember a lot of cousins, from Manchester, came to Granny's and we used to have a sing song, all the old songs and hymns. I used to think it was wonderful. I had a good time there, best time of my life until I got married.

I always enjoyed school. I liked it when we used to go out gardening, for lessons. Old Mr Jones was Welsh and was very very strict. Honor Dawson was a trainee teacher then . She married Mr Benton. When they were courting we used to watch them around and say 'Honor's after him again'. We used to weed in the garden and sow seeds in little pots. Two of the Durber brothers, they were devils, you know. They'd do anything to aggravate. Mr Jones used to get the cane out and slash them across their hands. As he tried to slash them they used to pull their hands back. Oh they were monkeys, those pair.

Granny died when I was thirteen and I had to go down to my dad. Dad's stepsister, Jane, lived with him, and I couldn't get on with her. I didn't stay long before I went out into service. I was in service till I got married.

I was just fourteen when I went to work at Heaton's. Where the club was there used to be a big house called Poolfields. There were three sisters: Miss Kate, Miss Mary and Miss Lydia. None of them were married. They ran a boarding school. They'd got a huge kitchen with teak tables and a piano in it. Miss Mary used to give piano lessons in the kitchen. I had to scrub the kitchen floor twice a day, and also the table. The children used to come in and, while I was scrubbing, Miss Mary was teaching the piano.

I had wanted to go into the mill but Dad had said no. He said I'd get in trouble. At Heaton's I used to get up about 5.30 to 6.00 in the morning and stayed up until they went to bed. If they wanted anything you had to be there. I started by lighting all the fires. I was young and I thought I was strong but I was no size. I was the only servant and had to wear a cap and apron. Part of the house was done off like classrooms. It was hard graft.

I lived in but not at the house. I had to cross the cobbled yard at night and my bedroom was in the row of cottages in front. It was the first one in the row and nobody lived downstairs.

The Goodwin family.
Left to Right:
Betty's mother Alice Goodwin nee Gibson, baby Nathan, Betty, Mark, John.

Betty and Harry Walklett on their wedding day 1935.

There came a girl once for a position there, at the house. I opened the door to her and asked her what her name was. I always remember to this day. She said 'I'm Miss Eliza Adams James'. I thought God, what a name! So I took her in and Miss Heaton interviewed her and gave her a job. She had to come and sleep in the same bed as me. She was a Northumberland girl. Well it didn't last long. She set fire to the bed, smoking, so of course that was her done for.

There was one little girl, at the school, called Chatfield. They were garage owners. She used to come every Monday morning, back from home and I'd be scrubbing or doing something. She'd come and put her arms round my neck and she used to love me up. I remember that little girl so well.

Miss Lydia, the middle one of the sisters, was the delicate one, but you could talk to her. Miss Mary was interested in the children, but Miss Kate was more like a man than a woman. She was a huge woman and used to take big strides when she walked.

Every other Sunday I had the afternoon off but, when I was in, I used to have to walk behind them to Brown Edge Church, on Sunday night: not with them, behind them. Well I got fed up with this and one Sunday I hid behind a gravestone and didn't go in. I thought 'I'm not going to do this anymore'. Later they asked me about the service and, as I couldn't tell them, I had to come clean. I told them that when I was a girl I was always sent to Heaton's Mission, at Hill Top. They said 'If you promise you'll go to the Mission, and not go home, we'll allow you to do that'. This is what I did. I couldn't stand walking up St Anne's Vale behind those two women. I was a bit of a rebel, I'm afraid. It was a lonely life there.

Miss Kate used to do the cooking but I used to help with draining the vegetables. One day I was emptying five pounds of potatoes. They were big iron saucepans in them days. I went to the sink and tipped it up and it went all over my foot and leg. I had black knit stockings on. Dr Davenport was sent for and he had to take this stocking off my scalded leg. I was a month at home and never went back. I couldn't do anything. I think they probably got somebody bigger and older. I felt so sorry when the house was knocked down, because it was part of my life. I say to my girls though 'It's no wonder I've got bad knees, I was down on my knees that much'.

I wandered from place to place, in service, and my dad always said 'If you make your bed you'll lie on it'. I used to say 'I watch I do lie on it as well'. My dad said hard things to me; about getting into trouble, which I'd no intention of doing anyway. I worked as a maid at Endon Hall once. It's been taken down now. It was a lovely big place with a big drive. There was only one other servant, she was Mrs Brown from Hill Top, and came in daily.

At all the places I worked I never earned more than ten shillings a week, except at the last one. I had sixpence to myself; I used to turn it all up to my dad.

I met my husband Harry when I was seventeen. I was courting for seven years. He was one of the best, I couldn't have had a better fellow. His mother was good to me too. She was more like a mother to me. I'd never known any real love, after Granny died, until then.

When I was married I was in service at Endon, a bungalow, with a family called Jackson. They treated me as one of their own. I loved it there. Mr Jackson was a surveyor. They gave me a lot of things when I got married and Mr Jackson lent us his car and chauffeur, who was Arthur Simcock. I have always lived in the same house, at Endon, since I was married.

Lorna Lovatt née Durber

I was born in 1936, in a cottage in Sandy Lane, now called Petra. My father, Daniel Durber, was born there too, in 1906. Grandfather, John Durber, bought the cottage when he was a young man. There was some ground with it and he had a stable at the side for a couple of horses. He had a pony and trap and used to take people to the stations at Endon and Stockton Brook.

Grandfather, John Durber, married Hannah Goodwin. Her mother kept the Foaming Quart pub. Dad was the youngest of seven but every other child died, at the age of about six months. There were six sons and one girl, Lucy, but only four sons survived. They were George, Harry, Fred and Daniel. I don't think Grandfather could read or write but he ended up teaching himself and became a fireman in the pit, at Whitfield.

Lorna's father Daniel on the horse, reins held by his brother Frederick. 1910c

Grandad's brother, Will, had a farm, Singlet House, and my dad went working there when he first left school. He only stayed about twelve months then he went working at Whitfield. He was only fourteen then. He later worked at Bellerton and Wolstanton; he ended up with a very bad chest and poor health.

My mother's name was May Counsel. She came from Leek and was the oldest of six. Mum and Dad had three children. A son Roy only lived 3 days. Then there was Alan and me. Alan died when he was forty-three.

Grandad owned the fields opposite our cottage and Uncle Fred had a house built there. It is now called Glenhough. He later rented it to Dad. We were all like one big family, with my cousins Rona, John and Ray. There used to be a little old cottage behind ours, where Underwoods now live. George Powell lived there, and there was a fire and he died. I think the paper lad found him, in the chair. It was thirty years ago. The fire had smouldered out but he had died from inhaling the smoke.

I went to Brown Edge School with my friend, Merle Tyler. We have been friends all our lives and went through school together, always in the same class. We were also big friends with Meda and Florence Adams. The playground then was only a dirt one and we used to build walls with it, make little rooms, and play houses. We were always having concerts, at playtime. I remember Merle used to do 'Burlington Bertie'; she always did that. There was a wall, all down the middle, separating our playground from the boys. I remember the boys snowballing us, over the wall. The toilets were still outside then.

A teacher, Miss Davenport, used to put a ring on her knuckle, and hit you in the back with it, if you didn't behave yourself. Mr Jennings was the headmaster, then it was Mr Fisher. I remember Miss Berrisford (later Mrs Durber) taught us how to knit.

Endon Secondary School trip to Babbacombe 1951.
The staff are seated. Mrs Benton is 7th from the left. Lorna Durber and Merle Tyler are on the back row towards the right.

Great Grandfather George Goodwin who lived at Fernyhough Farm. His wife Charlotte kept the Foaming Quart.

Great Grandmother Charlotte Goodwin

We went to Endon School, when we were eleven. I was always in the top class, I don't know why. Mrs Benton used to take us for sewing. If you'd tacked something up and you went to throw the bit of cotton away she'd say 'Don't throw that away, you can use that again, never throw anything away.' She was a very strict teacher. I don't know what she'd make of things today.

When we were growing up we had a lot of fun. We were never in, and parents never worried about where we were. We always seemed to have bad winters then, with snow and ice every year. We used to play in the Hollybush field and the one next to it, sliding down and sledging, every night. There always used to be loads and loads of kids. We used to spend hours up there, and it was dark, you know. I remember Derek Berrisford used to live in a cottage at the top of the fields then. He used to throw buckets of water down on the slides, at night, to make sure it stayed frozen.

Brown Edge Club used to be a wooden hut, where Sandy Lane Chapel is now. We used to go there twice a week for film shows. It was Reels on Wheels and I think it was George Nixon, from Newcastle, who did it. He called himself 'Nixon's Promotions'. It was always full. This was in the early fifties and it was about sixpence. If it broke down we always used to make a noise and stamp our feet. We used to go to the cinema at Smallthorne as well. I think it was called The Palace but we called it 'The Scratch'.

We always went to Sandy Lane Chapel. The Weaver family ran it and put their heart and soul into it. Another gentleman, called Albert Mountford, used to teach us as well. He was very nice. There were services on Sunday morning and evening and bible class in the afternoon. It was a real social place the chapel was. We had parties there doing spinning the plate etc. One night a week they used to have 'Sunshine Corner'; Cissie and Alan Hawley used to run it. I suppose it was just a gathering for a natter and a few games. We always used to sing:

Sunshine Corner, oh it's jolly fine
It's for children under ninety-nine.

Grandparents John and Hannah Durber nee Goodwin. Hannah suffered with arthritis. This would have been taken outside the cottage in Sandy Lane.

BELOW:
Procession at the end of World War II.
Back Row left to right: Snape, ?, Mary Brailsford, Rona Durber
Front Row left to right: Beryl Morgan, Bertha Clements, Lorna Durber

BELOW:
St Anne's School Prefects 1946.
Back L to R: Brian Proctor, Derek Jervis, Lorna Durber, Mavis Ford, Stanley Simcock
Front L to R: Miriam Pointon, Doreen Finney, Mr Fisher, Anne Dawson, Florence Adams.

All are welcome, seats are given free
Brown Edge Sunshine Corner is the place for me

Merle, me and the Adams twins always used to go to the Band Room on a Saturday night. Mr Arkinstall played his records and he always dressed up, with a dicky bow on, you know, as if he was at the Albert Hall. He called himself 'Jimmy Arkinstall and his Black Discs'. There was a circular thing with coloured cellophane on, a bulb behind and a handle. Mr Arkinstall used to put a record on, then give it a twirl and it flashed lights on the walls and ceiling - our first disco. It was still packed then, people came from all over. It was Glen Miller style music. I wrote a poem about the Band Room, which says it all. I remember, during the war, we had to go to the Band Room to try our gas masks on. All the boys kept making rude noise inside theirs. We had to carry the gas masks everywhere with us.

Jimmy Arkinstall who provided the music in the Band Room, on Saturday nights. He played records and took over from the Sherratt's Band. He called himself "Jimmy Arkinstall and his Black Discs"!

I left school at fifteen and went to work at Bullers at Milton, doing fettling. Afterwards I went to Brough, Nicholson & Hall at Leek, who made fringing, on big machines. I married Lol in 1956, at Brown Edge Church, and had my reception at the 'TAB'. Mr Benton did the photographs for us. I still live on Brown Edge, not far from where I was born. Here is my Band Room poem for your amusement:

Down to the Band Room on Saturday's we'd sway
One and six at the door we'd pay.
The powder room, that's the first stop
Have I got measles, no this mirror's got spots.
Small girls at the front, standing on tips,
tall girls at the back, painting petal, pink lips
Is that Evening in Paris or Goya Gardenia
Dab some more, the smell from this loo, you're never quite sure
Out on the dance floor, candle wax shine
I'm not much for yours, I'd rather have mine
Down the length of the room sat the girls, at the sides
The boys, round the pot stove, all best suits and smiles
We'd waltz round that floor like Victor Sylvester
With Arkinstall's lights, each night a fiesta
Too soon it's all over, tracks home to be made
But, not before the last waltz and moonlight serenade
If I'm honest you know, it was a bit of a dump
But just the thought of that place, my throat gets a lump
It was our palais de dance and our Albert Hall
Not very posh, just magic, that's all.

Brown Edge Church Choir 1971.
Back Row L to R: Rev. E. Rastall, Ray Amos (choirmaster), Bert Pointon, ?, John Worthy
3rd Row L to R: ?,?,?, Sheila Amos, Diane Cooper, ?, Miss Snape, Martin --
2nd Row L to R: ?, Jackie Snape, Jill Pickstock, Miss Huxley, Janet Turner
Front Row L to R: Karen Lovatt, 3 of the Jones Family, ?, Miss Stevenson, Louise Harvey.

A holiday at Blackpool c.1949.
Back L to R: ?, ?, Harry Turner, Ray Simcock, Fred Rolinson, Roy Berrisford, Billy Dale, ?, ?, Roy Turner, Ken Bassnett, Ian Adams.
Middle row L to R: Jack Bourne, Raymond Durber, Mavis Bassnett, ?, ?, Mrs Shaw, Emmie Bourne, ?, Nancy Simcock, ?.
Front L to R: June Bourne, Cynthia Bassnett, Betty Cope, Barbara Harrison, Nellie Pepper, Nora Sherratt, Sylvia Shaw, John Bourne

Granny Caroline Sherratt - Elizabeth Menzies née Sheldon

Nellie Sheldon (nee Gratton) the mother of Elizabeth Menzies, with two of her other children, Jack and Rene.

I was born in Short Street, Sandy Lane in 1916. My parents were John William and Nellie Sheldon; my father's family nickname was 'Snip'. My mother's maiden name was Gratton. Mother did not have very good health so my Granny (Dad's mother) reared me from three weeks old. Granny Caroline was born in 1851 and she always said she was born on a boat, at Great Haywood.

Granny's parents were Joseph and Sheba (Sabra) Bowyer, of Fiddlers Bank. Great Grandfather Joseph was a boatman on the canals. Granny said that she herself had had thirteen children, but six of them died. Her first husband Josiah (Jesse) Sheldon died when he was forty-six. He was kicked by a pit pony, at Whitfield Colliery. Her second husband was Ephraim Sherratt.

Granny Caroline was right old fashioned, but she would never have anything said against me. I was her pride and joy and there was nobody like 'Her Liz'. She wasn't soft with me though, she was very strict. She was a well-known character on the village, with her shawl and cloth bonnet. She always smoked a clay pipe., She used to smoke twist - what miners used to smoke; she cut it up and rubbed it in her hands first, before putting it in the pipe.

We lived at the Foaming Quart. I used to clean the red quarry floors on my hands and knees at six o'clock in the morning. Granny slept in the same bedroom as me. We had a big iron bedstead, a little blowlamp for a light and a brick in the bed, to warm us.

I used to have to go to school in clogs. I used to tuck my skirt over my belt so I could have a short skirt like the other girls. My granny made me have long wool things on, made out of one of her old gowns, black stockings and these great big clogs. I used to hide my white shoes in the wall, and put 'em on, then come back and change into me clogs, before I went home.

Granny used to give me sandwiches to take to school on Mondays, when it was washday. It was an all day job then - dolly tub, fires going, boiling. We ate in the classroom. The

Mrs Caroline Sherratt. She was the eldest child of Joseph and Sheba Bowyer who lived in a cottage on Fiddlers Bank. Her first husband was Jesse Sheldon and after his death she married Ephram Sherratt.

Elizabeth Sheldon, as a young
woman 1933.

teacher shouted at me and said I couldn't have my dinner, because I hadn't brought a tablecloth, to put over the desk.

I went home and Granny said, 'What are you doing here?' I said 'The teacher's sent me back 'cos I haven't got a tablecloth for on the desk.' Well Granny puts her shawl on and her bonnet on her head, a cloth one with a frill at the bottom. 'Come on.' she says. So we go down to school and all the kids are eating their dinners. She says to the teacher. 'What's up about my wench with no tablecloth on the table. It's only dirty buggers as have cloths. On my table you eat on a bloody scrubbed-top table, you can eat off it, never mind a bloody cloth.' Granny then said to me 'Now sit ye down and get your snappin eaten.'

At dinnertime, at school, some of the lads used to go fishing. One day, I stood up in assembly and some lad put fishes down my back. I screamed out, because they were live fishes. The teacher came to fetch me out and hit me. I went home and fetched Granny. She said to the teacher, 'You bloody touch my Lizzie again and I'll take that bloody head off your shoulders!'

One day the sewing teacher told us to bring things to patch. She said to me 'Elizabeth, you must ask your Grandma to give you something to bring tomorrow, for patching.' I told Granny and she gave me this nightgown and it was full of patches already, all over. I said, 'I'm not taking that', it seemed so poor. 'You'll bloody take that,' she said. So I took it and the teacher comes round the desk, looking at what we'd got. She took mine off me and took it to the front of the class. She held it up - this big white calico gown, full of patches. The teacher said 'Now look at this, this is very industrious, all these patches. That's good, throwing nothing away.' There she was praising me up. All the others had taken nice posh things with a little hole in. I don't think there was room for another patch on my gown I'd taken.

As I got older I felt more embarrassed. I always stood on the stage at Chapel and always had to sing solo. The Chapel was full, it was jam-packed. Granny had come at night, and you could see her above everybody else, with this big black bonnet. She always had a black velvet thing round her neck 'cos she had a carbuncle. Well I'm standing on stage and Granny was shouting out. She was deaf you know. She shouted, 'That's my wench - that's my Liz that one there - that one with the white hair'. I was so embarrassed. 'She sings like a lark', shouts Granny.

I went to Brown Edge Club with her once; it was the pensioner's Christmas party. She stood on top of the table singing 'The Old Short Clay' with her pipe in her hand. She never had any teeth in, I'd never known her have any in.

Granny took me to the Hippodrome in Burslem, once. It was live theatre and we sat on wooden seats. I was only very small and I couldn't see. 'What's up?' says Granny. 'I can't see,' I replied. ;It's that bloody woman in front with that hat on,' says Granny. She pokes the woman and says 'Take that bloody hat off, my wench conna see.' The woman turns round and says, in a posh voice 'Try not to do that will you. I'm not taking my hat off for you, or anybody.' Granny gets her stick, gets the hat and flings it down in the aisle. 'Now get your bloody hat then,' she says.

Granny Caroline with her husband Ephram Sherratt.
Caroline died in 1936, aged 85 years.

When I had a cold, or anything, Granny used to fetch the Guinness out, put the poker in it, and sprinkle it with ginger. She made me drink that. When I had a cough at night, she used to come with the goose oil fat and rub me chest. She made me a rabbit skin coat out of rabbit skins. It was like a waistcoat and I had to wear it next to me chest, tied there. I had to wear that when I went to school, under my liberty bodice, three flannelette petticoats, then me old-fashioned frocks. Doctors used to come to school sometimes and we had to wait, in turn, to be examined. They used to go mad at all the clothes I'd got on.

When I was older Gran said I was a 'brazen bugger' when I wore a backless dance dress. 'You'll catch ye bloody death of cold,' she said. She gave me a paper full of treacle toffee once, when I was going to a dance, to keep the cold off.

When Granny left the Foaming Quart one of her sons and his wife took over. Granny and Grandad went to live in a wooden bungalow at the bottom of Hough Hill, below the pub.

They used to come for Granny sometimes, if someone had died, and she used to go to lay them out. She told us once about a woman 'who wasn't all there'. This woman sent for Granny when her husband died. When Gran went round, the woman was sitting by the fire, taking no notice. 'Well where is he then?' says Gran. 'You'll find him upstairs,' says the woman. It was all dark and Granny tripped over the body on the floor and banged her head on the fender. She went back downstairs and said to the woman, 'I want some clean things for him.' 'He had em on a Sunday,' replied the woman. He obviously wasn't having any more!

My mother had moved from Sandy Lane up to The Rocks to Rock House. When Grandad died Granny went to live with Mother. Granny Caroline died in 1936, aged 85. The doctor said there was nothing wrong with her - it was just old age.

Granny was such a character. I have always remembered her and I've told these stories, many times, to my family.

Elizabeth Menzies died in 2005. These memories were taped by her family a few years before she died. It seemed obvious to her family that Granny Caroline imparted to Elizabeth her strength of character, and it served her well through her adult life.

Elizabeth Menzies (nee Sheldon) aged 87.
She died in 2005

Grace Hewitt née Dawson

I was born at Mission Cottage, Hill Top in 1909. I shall be 97 in July. My granny was a Charlesworth. My father was James Dawson and my mother was Ethel Lowe before she was married. Mother's father was Frederick Lowe. We lived just above Charlesworth's Mission and always went there for Sunday services. I remember the Charlesworth sons, standing all in a row, and they used to sing in harmony. It was lovely and I shall always remember that as long as I live. The Mission had a tent once in our field and we went on stage there. We'd all got our white frocks on and everyone left their straw hats in our parlour.

The Mission was only a tin thing then. My mother used to clean it. When they had christenings we used to take a basin of water down. The bungalows weren't there then. My husband, Norman, built those.

Granny Dawson lived at the end of Marshes Hill, in Back Lane, when I was a girl. It was a lovely house and they were very nice people. My father was the only one that drank. He was good looking but he was always drinking. I hate pubs, you know. Mother and father had six children: Jonathon, Frederick, and the twins George Reginald and Robert William. Then there was me and Doris.

Dad was a miner and his father before him. His father, Jonathon Dawson, was killed at work, at Whitfield. He was forty-two.

I was in the girl guides at Brown Edge. Miss Lawton, the Vicar's daughter, was the boss and we met in Church House. They used to take us swimming after school. We used to have to walk to Burslem and back. Eva Proctor used to take us as well. She was a lovely person: Oh, those were the days.

Miss Lawton used to take us down to Greenway Hall at Knypersley. We walked down there, through the fields, and had tea on the lawn there.

My friend Madge Proctor and I got the sack from the guides. They told us to clean the grate in Church House and black lead it, and we wouldn't do it; it was a lark you know.

When I was at school I remember Mrs Proctor, when she taught us. She was lovely she was. The headmaster, Mr Jones, was vile. If you weren't behaving he used to throw the chalk at you. When it was Pancake Day we used to have a half-day off school.

The Lowe family who lived at Hill Top.
Back L to R: Grace's mother Ethel, Beatrice and Hilda.
Front row L to R: Grandfather Frederick Lowe, Frank Moss, Grandmother Harriet Lowe.

We always used to walk down to Endon School, through the fields. Mr Heaton, that posh man, left money for widows and their children. We used to take a pillowslip down and we were given four loaves. If you were a widow you had half a crown. They used to call your name out for the bread. My mother hated that. She said it was bad enough being poor.

I was in the Girl's Friendly Society at Miss Heaton's. All Endon lot used to come up, swanky lot. When I was about twelve I was in a concert called 'A needle in a haystack' at the new Mission. It was lovely.

On Sunday afternoon I used to go with my granny to the Heaton's at Poolfield House. We used to go through the double gates and to a little room on its own, up a courtyard. There were about a dozen of us and we used to sing and say prayers. I used to love it.

We used to fetch our water from the well where Jacker Berrisford lived. We had all our groceries from Gibson's little shop, near the Colliers Arms. Mrs Higgins also had a shop, in a little hut, at the New Mission. I remember she had a notice on the wall, which said, 'Please do not ask for trust; a refusal may offend.' She was a right stern one, Mrs Higgins.

I had scarlet fever when I was fifteen and was very bad. They came to fetch me with a horse and trap. Black Maria they called it. I think it was Mr Bentley. They took me to the Isolation Hospital in Tinster's Wood. Mrs Bentley was the nurse and Mr and Mrs Bentley lived in the house by the hospital. They were very nice though.

Grace aged ten.

I was very frightened. I had sciatica with it, and a terrible throat. When you have scarlet fever you peel and your skin comes off. There was a girl in the next bed, called Phoebe, and she was very bad and died. I can always remember Elsie Bourne, from Top Heath Row was in with me. There were about fifteen beds and there was two in a bed then.

Visitors would come at certain times and look at you through the window. My dad came every day. He used to come when he shouldn't and stand on this path and wave at me. Mrs Bentley said to my mother, 'Mrs Dawson, does he think a lot about Grace, he's always here!!' I was in for six weeks. They called my dad 'Sour' - that was our nickname - but he loved children.

When I left school at thirteen, I went to work at Wardle and Davenport at Leek, on hosiery. It was a very strict place. If you were late you got locked out and had to go home.

I worked on 'Three Knots' stockings, which were the best ones you could wear. We used to sit round this table and we used to sing, hymns mostly. We had to put the stockings inside out over our hand and cut all the little bits off with a pair of scissors. The stockings were white cotton ones and they were knitted on a machine and then sent to the dye house, down Mill Street. Seaming was the best-paid job.

I used to get up at 5:30 and boil the kettle on the fire for a drink, and do a piece of toast. I walked down to Endon Station with Nellie Sheldon, to catch the train at seven o'clock, to Leek. We walked up to Wardle and Davenports and waited outside until it opened at 7:45 am. We finished at 5:45 pm and had to do all that back again. What a life! I had the sack once; I think I'd been laughing. Our boss, Mr Bryan, said, 'You were talking and not looking at your work. Get off home'. I was suspended for three days. I told everybody I'd got a sore throat.

I married Norman Hewitt, at Endon Church, when I was twenty-two. He was a builder. When war came Norman went into the army and I worked at the munitions factory at Radway Green. It was the simplest job in my life. We all sat round a table, talking and laughing. We had a disc of metal with a hole in it, and we had to put another piece of metal in the hole, to see if it fitted; it was for guns. We then put them in a box, the ones that were done. It was pretty good wages and we worked shifts.

Grace with her husband, Norman Hewitt, and son Rex. This was taken at Southport in 1931.

My husband was a prisoner of war. I had a letter saying he was missing, then two months later, a letter said that he was a prisoner, at Stalag 357 Camp. He was captured at the Battle of Anzio and was a prisoner for three years.

He came home on the train to Burslem and then caught the bus home. He couldn't get home quick enough. He was terribly ill; what a wreck. He could hardly stand up and you couldn't tell him. He couldn't sleep on a bed; he had to lie on a board. He couldn't eat and he couldn't sleep. The neighbours were good. I had a hundred eggs given to me, to build him up, and Horlicks. He got sick of Horlicks; he said he never wanted to see Horlicks again. I looked after him and they fixed for him to go to a holiday camp in Blackpool.

He picked up and started bricklaying again, but he was never the same. He was more bad-tempered. He died in 1969, at the age of fifty-nine.

Norman Hewitt, Grace's husband. He was captured at the Battle of Anzio and was a prisoner of war for three years.

Grace is pictured with three other helpers who worked for Mrs Crossley's catering business.
L to R Grace, Alice Proctor, Alma Proctor, Ethel Roberts.

Alan Hayes

I was born at The Roebuck pub, in 1936. My dad was Horace Hayes and my mum was Lottie Grindy, before she was married. Dad originated from Ilam and was in farm service at Rudyard when he met me mum. In them days Rudyard was like a local Blackpool. I think Mum was born at Bank End, Brown Edge, and there were three sisters and a brother. The brother, Bill Grindy, built Thelma Avenue.

The Roebuck public house. Note the Parker's Ales sign and also the side entrance which used to be opposite Bratt's Butchers. This building is now Keith's workshop. Lottie Hayes on left, Louie Pointon on the right.

Mum and Dad moved into the Roebuck in the thirties, and kept it for thirty-three years. It was quite a nice place to grow up in, there was plenty going on. I grew up listening to them singing all the old songs in the smoke room and went to bed listening to 'Roll out the Barrel'.

I had to help out. I used to have one horrible job and I cringe when I think about it now. They used to have cast iron spittoons, with sawdust in, and they were shoved under the seats. As I was small I could crawl under the seats and get 'em out and empty them. All the miners smoked. If we didn't open the landing window, you had a job to see upstairs; it was like a smog.

We did not have a liquor licence at first, it was just beer. It was hard keeping the beer cool in them days; we had to chuck buckets of cold water over it, in the cellar. As you went into the pub the smoke room was on the left and this was Mum's end. The lounge bar was on the right and that was Dad's. There was always fighting outside - just a bit of scrapping.

Dad was mates with Sam Bratt and went to the market with him on Wednesdays. I could go on all day about Sam. He used to go in the shop and buy a jar of sweets for us kids. He owned the field below Varsovia and he used to mow it. There'd be a gang of us lads there. He used to go up in his Daimler car and he'd tie a big tarpaulin on the back. We'd load all the hay on this tarpaulin and he'd come over by the gate and put it in a haystack. At the end of the day he'd stick us all on this tarpaulin and go round the field like hell, swinging us all off, at the back of the Daimler. That was Sam all over.

When the war came, we saw a lot of servicemen coming in and out of the pub. One day dad said, 'Come look at Sam Hancock's two sons!' They sat by the front door and they were in their guard's dress uniform. They were great big tall lads and very smart. We never saw them again. Uncle Edgar Burrows, from Willfield Lane, organized a fund for the servicemen. The pub raised money and when the men came home, they were given five shilling, sometimes ten. You could get drunk in them days on five shillings, drunk as a monkey. All the names and amounts were recorded in a book, which I still have.

Mum and Dad used to do their little bit for the church, when they had a Harvest Home, at the pub. People used to bring all the stuff and it was auctioned off. It went on for a good many years and they raised quite a lot of money. It was funny because they used to get all the locals in, like Harvey Durber, and my grandad, and the Vicar amongst them. There was lots of singing 'All is safely gathered in' and all that.

Harvest Service at The Roebuck, c.1962.
L to R: George Hall, Arthur Sherratt, Sam Jervis, Horace Hayes, Betty Mitcheson, ?.
Note the jar of brylcream at the back - always the first item to be auctioned.

The first item to be auctioned was always a jar of Brylcream. Dad, being bald and just being mischievous, used to bid for this. If there was anybody, else in, with a bald head, they used to run him up and he'd end up paying too much for it.

A lot of Americans used to come, from Blackshaw Moor, in their jeeps. They used to park outside the Lump of Coal and get as drunk as monkeys, with three pubs and a club so close. 'Got any gum chum?' we used to say to them. When the jeeps were parked up we used to go and tie a tin can underneath and then listen to it banging as they went down Clay Lake.

At one time the Brass Band practised in a red brick building attached to the pub. We called them the 'Ale and Bacca Band'. It was fantastic on Christmas morning, because the Band used to go all round the village and end up at our pub, playing and having a drink. A team of hand bell ringers used to come round as well, with George Hall and Bob Cumberlidge. You don't get it now; it used to be great.

Dad bought a field off Alan Pointon, which is now Keith's car park. It used to be called Malkin's meadow. Dad used to breed poultry, as a sideline, and had incubators with about four thousand eggs.

The New Inn was next door. It was a big place and used to have a police cell at one time. Chadwick's lived there when we were kids. I worked on knocking it down with Harold Bourne, the builder.

I remember a woman we used to call 'Sixpence Halfpenny Florrie' who used to live in Back Lane. She used to fancy herself as a policewoman like, and used to stand at the halt sign, by Bratt's shop, directing traffic. She had a policeman's uniform on, and it was funny because there'd only be a car then about every half hour.

We had a lot of fun, as kids. We used to go scrumping apples at Poolfields House where Heaton's lived. It used to be lovely down the Breach, before the miner's houses were built. There were chestnut trees and a brook on the left. I've spent hour's conkering down there. There used to be a pool at the bottom, opposite Stephen Buckley's house, probably where Poolfield House got its name. The house used to look toward Rock Cottage and had a well-built stone wall round it and railings. As lads we used to peer through the gates at the front of the house. Jim Davenport, at the farm behind, used to run us lads many times. The best way to the orchards was at the back, by the farm.

Once we were playing at the back of the Club and we heard this big bang. Somebody said there was a plane crash, up Wood

Arthur Davenport on his smallholding behind the Lump of Coal, Cross Edge.

Bank. We set off up there. You didn't have to ask your mother, in those days, if you could go - we just went. I think it was an American Liberator, a bomber. I can see Sam Bratt now, running up and down. He'd got his white butcher's slop on and was just trying to get folk out of it. It was all in flames. I've never seen anything written about it. There was a lot of people up there.

During the war I had a Mickey Mouse gas mask, a red one. George Berrisford was the same age as me, and we used to go up school together, but he was a lot bigger than me. He still remembers being envious of me because he had to have 'a bog standard black gas mask'.

Barrage balloons were massive things and were used to stop bombers getting low. They had them on a great big cable. One day one must have broke loose from somewhere and it came over Brown Edge. It came up St Anne's Vale, the cable trailing, and up Old Lane. Someone managed to get hold of it, near Little Stonehouse and fastened it to a gatepost.

As lads, we used to go fishing down the back of Upper Stonehouse, down to the feeder. We used to catch red penks and fat hens. We'd be gone all day. We made our own fishing nets out of mother's stockings. We used to get a bit of wire and shove it in the end of a cane. We would have a jam jar tied with a piece of string, to make a handle. Fifty per cent of the time you'd get back to the church and the string would fall off, the jam jar would break, and all the fish would be lying in the road.

As kids we all had our little areas. We were Sandy Laners, Jobs Pool were Rocksers (because of the Rocks). There were School Bankers, Sytchers and Hilltoppers. We used to play football on Hollybush fields and Barry Proctor used to run us.

Dad was in the army, in London, in the Artillery. He was stationed in Scotland once though and was part of the guard over Hesse, when the German crash-landed there. Dad died at the age of sixty-one and Grandad died at sixty-one, so I was glad when I got past that.

I married Sylvia Pugh and we later had a bungalow built on our land, called Brookside. It had half an acre with it. My daughter had a pony on the field where Keith's car park is now. We lived there until about 22 years ago and then I bought Star Farm.

Star Farm, on Marshes Hill, is a very old place and Star Well is on our land. They say the farm used to be an old drover's inn, dating back to the 1600s. It is on the old route from Leek to Biddulph. It's said the drovers put their cattle on the field at the front, while they came in for a drink. John Goodwin is a big metal detector man and he's had more old coins out of this field than anywhere he's been. It must have been a remote area up here in them days.

I had always lived down the village but I always had the feeling that I wanted to be high up. The views are amazing here, you can see for miles, all around.

The British Legion Queen and retinue c.1942.
PC Evans is on the top left of the picture.
The queen is Beryl Hancock and Alan Hayes is the page boy. Trainbearers are Irene Hughes, Beryl Hulland, Joyce Dawson, Marie Turner, May Taylor, N. Evans.
Front L to R:
?, ?, Ann Dawson, Margaret Wright, Mavis Foster, Joy Willott, ?, Freda Cunliffe, ?, Carol Paddock.

The Roebuck Darts Team B.
L to R: Ernie Pointon, Bill Merrick, Enoch Heath, Dennis Machin, Les Cunliffe, Jim Mellor, Frank Harrison, Jim McLean, Joe Bourne, Horace Hayes.

The Roebuck Darts Team A.
L to R: Morris Heath, Alan Hayes, Richard Pugh, Lottie Hayes, Fred Simcock, Dinah Pointon, Horace Hayes, Bill Burrows, John Fowler.

ABOVE: 'All is safely gathered in'
at The Roebuck 1960.
Back row L to R: Reg Twemlow, ?,
?, Dennis Mosedale, Herbert
Bourne, Bill Sellars.
Seated L to R: Horace Hayes, Lottie
Hayes, Rev R G Lansdale, ?.

A pint at The Roebuck, 1959.
Left to right: Sam Jervis, Jim
Grindy, Harry Durber, Harvey
Durber, Bill Rowley.

The vicar leads the singing at
The Roebuck, c.1960.
Left to right: Harry Durber,
Harvey Durber, Rev R G
Lansdale, Bill Rowley, Sam
Selby, Bill Protheroe.

Another Harvest picture at the Roebuck, c.1961.
Back left to right:
Rev. E H B Richards, ?.
Sylvia Hayes, Horace Hayes.
Front left to right:
Sam Hancock, Sam Jervis.

Tramps again in The Roebuck.
Back row L to R: Mr Clements, Horace Hayes, Denis Mosedale, ?, Lottie Hayes, Dinah Pointon, Harry Hammond, Joe Cumberlidge.
Front row L to R:
Reg Twemlow, ?, Chris Hargreaves, ?.

The Roebuck regulars dressing up again, c.1961. The tramps in the Landrover are *left to right*: Denis Mosedale, Horace Hayes Chris Hargreaves, Reg Twemlow.
This is taken in Sandy Lane outside Tyler's Shop and the tramps were off to The Mermaid Pub.

Foster's Row - Ted Foster

They call it Top Chapel Lane now but it was known also as Foster's Row, because there were numerous Fosters there - four families and all relatives. Two brothers, Jack and Tom Foster married two sisters, Jane and Ellen Pickford, from Leek,

I was born in 1929. My dad was Tom Foster and my mother was Ellen Pickford. I was the youngest of ten, right down the bottom. Everything that was handed down, I ended up with. We slept top to bottom, three or four in a bed. My dad was strict.

I don't remember my grandparents; they were dead before I was born. I do know Dad was born at the end of the row, in the cottage at the top of the steps, from New Lane. Grandfather was a coal haulier, with a horse and cart. There are generations of Fosters in the churchyard.

A coal haulier down St Anne's Vale early 1900s.

We always went to the Free Mission. When I was about ten I used to pump the organ up. If I didn't like the hymn I stopped pumping. You used to have to go to Chapel then - they wanted you out of the way.

Dad was a miner at Whitfield. All through the thirties there was no work, that was the sad part about that. You'd hear the blower go at Whitfield, and the miners all turned out to go.

When they got there they were treated like cattle. They'd say we've got work for you, you and you. The miners had trudged down all that way, two and half miles, with their water and snappin tin. They'd walk all the way back and have to try again the next day. Unbelievable isn't it? I was determined not to go in the mines. I started work in a mill at Leek when I was fourteen.

The older villagers still call it Foster's Row but there are no longer any of these families living there.

Judith Hodkinson, nee Sheldon and her brothers, Spencer sitting and Oliver in the centre. This was taken in the field opposite New Lane Farm. Top Chapel Lane (Foster's Row) is in the background. The house is the one at the end of the lane, where Ted Foster's father was born.

Pupils at Endon School, c.1940. Judith Hodkinson is on the 2nd row, first right.

Endon Pupils c.1940.

New Lane Farm - Judith Hodgkinson née Sheldon

My father, Jesse Sheldon, was born in St Anne's Vale: the first cottage after the churchyard. He was one of nine children and his parents were Jacob and Eliza Sheldon. My mother's name was Sarah Buckley before she married. When Dad bought New Lane Farm, it was just a little cottage, with a very low roof. He modernized it and raised the roof. It was a smallholding of twenty acres.

A recent photo of New Lane Farm. Centre front is where the standpipe was.

He was a miner at Black Bull, but he eventually got enough livestock to give up his job. He had about twelve to fourteen milking cows and he kept a lot of pigs and hens. He delivered eggs up Smallthorne bank, to the little shops there, two or three times a week. He used to go to Parker's brewery, in Burslem, to fetch his grains for the cattle.

The people from the cottages above, in Foster's Row and Chapel Lane, used to come and fetch milk from us. The rest of the milk went to Nestles, in Congleton. They came to pick it up in the churns.

Hill Top did not have piped water until 1937. We had a stand tap outside and it was as far as the mains water came to. So people from Chapel Lane and Top Chapel Lane came every day to fetch water from our tap.

When I married Alec Hodgkinson we went to live at East View, Hill Top. My brother, Oliver, carried on here when our parents died. The ground was rented out then, as Oliver worked for the Council. Later, when Oliver died, I came back to live at the farm. I have come back to where I was born, New Lane Farm.

New Lane Farm. On the right is Sarah Sheldon, nee Buckley. Mr Hugh Henshall Williamson had New Lane constructed in about 1846. It was to make it easier for his coach and horses when travelling from Greenway Bank to St Anne's Church.

Jacob Sheldon ,who lived in the first cottage in St Anne's Vale, and Eliza Sheldon, his wife

Granny's Heath's Shop
- Jean Whitfield née Mayer

My Grandma was Sarah Heath. Her maiden name was Sheldon and her parents were Jacob and Eliza Sheldon. They lived in the first cottage in St Anne's Vale, next to the churchyard. Eliza died in 1914 and Jacob in 1928. Gran was in service at Endon and later married William Heath from Biddulph Moor. They had three children.

Grandma's sister Polly (her real name was Mary) worked in service, at the Vicarage, from when she was thirteen to eighteen. It was Rev. Young then. She always said that she got fifteen shilling a quarter. She lived in the Coach House, which she called the Lichgate house.

Aunt Polly later lived at Rock End, Biddulph Moor. She was ill for

Sarah Heath outside her shop in St Anne's Vale c.1938.

Sarah Sheldon, on the left, when she was in service. Sarah was the daughter of Jacob and Eliza. She married William Heath.

The Heath Family.
L to R: Joseph, Sarah, Donald, William and Clarice.

Clarice Heath aged seventeen.

Clarice Mayer nee Heath with her mother, brother and daughter, c.1942. *L to R:* Clarice, Donald, Sarah and Jean.

two years and her husband, Uncle Joe Edge, asked Grandma if she would go and look after her. He told her whatever she got in service he would pay her. So Gran finished in service and that's what she did. That is how she came to meet Grandad, as he lived at Biddulph Moor.

When Grandad died, in about 1938, Granny opened the little shop to give herself some income. She went to see Mrs Hollins at her shop and asked if, when the traveller came with the sweets, she would send him round.

She had the shop in the front room at first, then Uncle Jack Pointon, on School Bank, built a wooden shed for her. She sold bread (a penny a loaf) sweets, paraffin, stamps, pies and lots more. She kept the shop until 1943 when she died at the age of fifty-seven.

I was born in my granny's cottage in 1939. I still live in St Anne's Vale, in a bungalow. I have lived in The Vale all my life, apart from three years when I was first married.

Tommy Powell's Place - Ted Foster

Tommy Powell's place was a large corrugated tin shed. It was on the corner of Sytch Road and High Lane. It was a filling station and Tommy also sold numerous spare parts for cars, motorbikes and cycles etc.

There was a narrow path down the middle of the shed and everything was piled high, on both sides, floor to ceiling. There was that much junk. Only Tommy knew where anything was. You had to wait half an hour before he found what you wanted, but he always had it.

He also charged up accumulators for radio sets. The petrol pump was worked by hand, and people used to keep him talking so he lost count. They got extra petrol then. He was a small, fat man with a limp – war injury I think. He always wore greasy overalls and a flat cap. He lived in the house next to the shed. If he was closed and you ran out of paraffin, you could always knock on his door.

During the war Tommy had cigarettes, for special customers – Park Drive and Woodbine cigarettes were always hidden underneath somewhere. He always told rude jokes and you could hear him laughing right up the road.

Tommy's place closed in the mid-fifties and a new bungalow now stands on the site – gone but not forgotten.

Well Dressing and Carnivals

According to the late Alan Pointon, Mr Jessie Sheldon and Mr James Pointon, both miners, first dressed the Spout Well, in Sandy Lane, in 1921. It was part of the Hospital Saturday effort for that year. It continued until about 1950, when Joy Weaver was the Village Hall Queen. She remembers it being the last well dressing.

This old tradition, of Well-dressing, was revived again 50 years later, in 2000 for the Millennium. We even made the Midlands TV News. Three wells are dressed now: The Spout, Sytch Road and Job's Pool, the latter dressed by the school.

The well-dressing is part of the Brown Edge Festival, held each year in July, along with the crowning of the Church Queen.

We have a team of well-dressers, who started with no experience. Anyone interested is always welcome.

Spout Well dressed for the Royal Jubilee in 2002, and designed by Adrian Mason.

RIGHT: The Well Dressing designer, Adrian Mason on the right and Allan Sims on the left, 2001. Allan was one of the main helpers, but he died in 2005. This picture was taken in his shippon at Hill Top Farm.

Spout Well, Sandy Lane in the early 1920s. It was dressed by Jesse Sheldon and James Pointon. The Chapel in the background was sold in 1980 and later demolished.

The Spout Well dressed, 1937.
The lady is Clarice Heath and the little boy
is Keith Hall.

Joy Weaver being given a drink from
the well by Rev. Ramsden, 1950.
This was the last time Spout Well was
dressed until 2000, when this old
tradition was revived.

The Queen and retinue c.1947.

The Queen and her retinue c.1947. The Queen is Joyce Dawson. This event took place in a field belonging to Spout House, where the miners' houses are now.

Maypole dancing in Spout Fields, c.1947. The teacher was Elsie Berrisford.

A group of Endon Secondary School pupils pictured at Spout Well, c.1949.
Back L to R: Marie Turner, ?, Florence Adams, Barbara Morten, Lorna Durber, Meda Adams, Merle Tyler, ?.
Middle L to R: Sheila Mould, Janet Hammond, Maureen Holland, Heather --, Margaret Hughes, Mavis Fowler,
Betty Smith, Graham Jervis, Audrey Cooper, Pam Leese, ?, ?, Margaret Ibbs, ?
Front L to R: Miss Cooper, Joan Smith, ?, ?, ?, Valerie Bettany

The Village Hall Queen, Joy Weaver, with her retinue 1950.
L to R: June Dutton, Betty Condliffe, Jean Mayer, Dorothy Weaver, Joy Weaver, Melvin Weaver, Clifford Doxey,
Chris Tatton, Margaret Hancock, Yvonne Weaver.
The three girls in bonnets are: Glenda Weaver, ?, Miss Simcock

The Wurzels Float, in the early 1970s.
L to R: Doreen Scott, Mabel Durber, Andrew Walker, Susan Watkin.
Front: Elizabeth Lawton.

An early Hospital Saturday photo of a policeman and Charlie Chaplin. The first Hospital Saturday was held on 4th August 1906. It was to raise money for North Staffordshire Infirmary.

The Church Carnival 1977c with fancy dress again. Adrian Lawton is the sweep and John Lawton is the packet of tea, which had a jump in price at this time – one of those 'panic buy' times.

The Young Wives float "Honolulu Splashdown". This was the year of the moon landing, 1969.
Back row left to right: Daphne Williamson, Elizabeth Lawton, Jennifer Salt, Audrey James, Janet Bourne.
Front row left to right: Elaine Picken, Elsie Hancock, Joyce Brereton, Evelyn Forrester.